Neil Evans is Director of M
He has served as a parish p
suburban west London. Before ordination he worked as
Service manager in Tower Hamlets. He has a doctorate in
Ministry and Theology from King's College London, in which
his main focus was the professional development of clergy.
He was born in Kent in 1954, is married and has two teenage
children.

SPCK Library of Ministry

Being a Chaplain
Miranda Threlfall-Holmes and Mark Newitt

Community and Ministry: An introduction to community
development in a Christian context
Paul Ballard and Lesley Husselbee

Developing in Ministry: A handbook for effective Christian
learning and training
Neil Evans

Finding Your Leadership Style: A guide for ministers
Keith Lamdin

How to Make Great Appointments in the Church:
Calling, Competence and Chemistry
Claire Pedrick and Su Blanch

Pioneer Ministry and Fresh Expressions of Church
Angela Shier-Jones

Reader Ministry Explored
Cathy Rowling and Paula Gooder

Reflective Caring: Imaginative listening to pastoral experience
Bob Whorton

Skills for Collaborative Ministry
Sally Nash, Jo Pimlott and Paul Nash

Supporting Dying Children and their Families:
A handbook for Christian ministry
Paul Nash

Supporting New Ministers in the Local Church: A handbook
Keith Lamdin and David Tilley

Tools for Reflective Ministry
Sally Nash and Paul Nash

Youth Ministry: A multi-faceted approach
Sally Nash

DEVELOPING IN MINISTRY

A handbook for effective Christian
learning and training

SPCK Library of Ministry

NEIL EVANS

First published in Great Britain in 2012

Society for Promoting Christian Knowledge
36 Causton Street
London SW1P 4ST
www.spckpublishing.co.uk

British Library Cataloguing-in-Publication Data
A catalogue record for this book is available from the British Library

ISBN 978–0–281–06398–7
eBook ISBN 978–0–281–06951–4

Typeset by Graphicraft Limited, Hong Kong
First printed in Great Britain by MPG Books
Subsequently digitally printed in Great Britain

eBook by Graphicraft Limited, Hong Kong

Produced on paper from sustainable forests

For my parents, Bob and Irene,
who nurtured me in my faith and who had faith in me

Contents

Contents

Foreword

For some ten years Neil Evans and I were occasional tutors on the now departed Aston Training Scheme for ministerial development. We used to play a little game of encouraging students and colleagues to guess which one of us was formed in the more catholic stable and which in the more evangelical. It amused us if nobody else, and we liked to think that the differences were hard to spot – for the reason that, whatever our ecclesial pedigrees, the intent and the method were the same. The intent was to see people formed as faithful and fruitful Christian disciples and ministers. The method, though probably neither of us then could have named it as such, was that which Neil now articulates and advocates so clearly in this book as organic and relational.

Neil tells us in this book that he finds doing research tedious but seems to come up with creditable results. If that is the case, then this work proves his point. Behind Neil's conclusions lies solid research based on the work of others and his own data collection. But rather more importantly, this work emerges out of many years as a proven practitioner in the field of developing people as disciples and ministers. This is, therefore, a book by a practitioner for practitioners. In relatively few pages it covers a wide range of both practice and theory, drawing on a variety of developmental and educational models. It has clear relevance to the work of developing ministers (both ordained and lay), and also much to say about the equally vital work of developing all Christian people in the vocation of being disciples in all parts of their living. Although emerging from and speaking mainly to a Church of England milieu, there is much here that will be relevant to those of other traditions.

Despite the Church of England focus, Neil has relatively little to say in this book about bishops – perhaps that is deliberate!

And yet much of the thinking that Neil shares with us is almost identical to that which I draw upon when reflecting on our model of *episcope* as exercised both by those who are formally bishops and by the many others with whom they share ministry. Indeed, as a slight aside, it is uncanny that, though we have not worked together in an active way for some years, I find myself reading here ideas and even particular phrases that I also hear myself using in my own reflection and teaching. Becoming a bishop eight years ago, the only way in which I have been able to approach the role has been to see it as essentially relational – the service for ordaining bishops tells us that they are 'to know their people and be known by them'. That relatedness to people leads (I fondly hope) to a ministry that takes seriously where people (lay and ordained, individually and collectively) are in terms of context and culture, and is thus able to equip, challenge and accompany them towards full and fruitful Christian living. Neil quotes the bishop who says, 'Ultimately I can't make the clergy do anything, but I can woo them.' Wooing is of course utterly relational, and it is indeed (in my view) only out of the reality of our relatedness to people that any of us who minister can hope to take our place in the work of developing those people whom God has given to us.

Rooting his thinking in the Trinitarian pattern of the inter-relatedness and interdependence of the Godhead, Neil gives us an approach to Christian development which is similarly shaped. This takes seriously the variety of people in terms of culture, tradition, giftedness, experience and personality preferences ('Jesus never invalidates a person's experience or situation'). It goes on to affirm the vocation to discipleship of all Christian people and the necessity of growing within the church a whole culture of development which expects people to want to develop. For the ordained, the developing of disciples is to be at the heart of their ministry; and so of course their own continuing development, vitality and relatedness to God are a sine qua non for the vitality of the whole Christian community and its mission.

Neil tells us that the clergy are not easily line-managed. For that I thank God (most of the time!) because within the church we are not primarily here to run an organization or manage people's performance against targets or criteria. We are here to see people formed individually and in community after the pattern of Christ. In Christ we are ourselves drawn into the dynamic and loving relatedness of the God who is Trinity. We take on the shape and nature of that God, being drawn also into the divine movement outwards to all creation which issues in the growing of God's kingdom. If this book helps us to help one another to develop thus as disciples and ministers, then the writing of it will have proved its value. I am confident that it will.

The Rt Revd James Langstaff
Bishop of Rochester

Acknowledgements

This book has been in formation over the years I have been involved in training, support and education in London Diocese and beyond. My gratitude, therefore, goes to many clergy and lay people who have taken part in the training and development in which I have been involved. I have learned a huge amount from them in the process.

However, I would particularly like to thank Martyn Percy who, as my doctoral supervisor, was a huge inspiration to the work which has formed a background to this book. I would also like to thank Michael Colclough, Pete Broadbent, Andy Windross, Rachel Treweek, Alan Gyle, Judy Barrett and so many clergy and lay colleagues in London who have been inspirational and supportive of the work and ministry which features in this book.

I am also grateful to James Langstaff, Nicola Slee, Stuart Mitchell and other colleagues with whom I have worked in training and development and who have informed my own development.

Finally, thanks to my sister Phyll Wood, who has read through the text for me, and to my family for their patience and understanding.

Abbreviations

CMD   Continuing ministerial development
*The Church of England's equivalent of CPD for
clergy and other formally recognized ministers*

CME   Continuing ministerial education
*Former term for CMD in the Church of England
(and still sometimes used)*

CPAS   Church Pastoral Aid Society
Church mission agency

CPD   Continuing professional development
*The generally accepted term for life-long learning and
development of those in professional roles and work*

MAP   Mission Action Plan
*A generic term of the church and parish planning
and vision process*

MDR   Ministerial development review
*Annual review process for Church of England clergy
(and other lay ministers). Roughly parallel to
appraisal in commerce, industry, professions, etc.,
but employed differently*

PCC   Parochial Church Council
*The 'governing body' of the local parish church in
the Church of England*

SHAPE   Spiritual gifts; Heart's desire; Abilities; Personality;
Experiences
*Acronym for vocational discernment course produced
by Carlisle Diocese*

SMART   Specific, Measurable, Achievable, Realistic, Timely
*Acronym for producing sharp objectives in a
planning process (see Appendix 2 for more detail)*

1

Introduction
Training and development that sticks

Christianity in the third millennium will essentially be, for the whole Church, the same as before – and yet totally different. It will be in its pure form the same faith, the same demand and the same gospel. But its expression must now be more internally varied and multi-dimensional, more experiential, more lay and more humble. Pray God, the Christian Church will thus become more *human*. It will have to accept variety, and acknowledge its plural humanity. Only in this way can it come closer to Christ.

(Astley 2007)

When I was a curate in Bethnal Green my training incumbent would invariably begin a Monday morning staff-meeting discussion about Sunday's sermon with the line, 'Good sermon, but what *difference* would it have made to people's lives?' It is a line that has stayed with me throughout my ministry. So often we are encouraged to attend courses or conferences, undertake training, read a book because somebody (other than ourselves) thinks it's a good idea: it'll be good for you. There can, of course, be a huge mismatch between what others think will be good for us and what we need – whether it's to develop in our Christian life, to do a job or ministry more effectively or simply to connect with our current situation.

In this book I shall be exploring ways in which we can put together training and development opportunities which can be as fruitful and effective as possible for participants; asking the question, 'What difference does it make?' I will be offering some tried and tested models alongside some clear guidelines based on research and experience.

One of the overwhelming themes that strikes me over and again in reading the Gospels is that Jesus began where people were, not where he thought they 'ought' to be. Jesus' parables were concerned with issues that people could readily relate to: sowing crops, caring for sheep, looking after someone who'd been mugged. When discussing issues with a lawyer or a Pharisee he used their language and starting point, but encouraged them to see further, to move on. So with fishermen, with the sick, with those caught up in the language of sin. Jesus never invalidated people's experience or situation, but always started from where they were and encouraged them to move on, beyond their situations and usually out of their comfort zone.

So it seems to me that a fundamental question that should always be asked of any training, education or development opportunity, whether it's continuing professional development for clergy or a baptism preparation course for the unchurched, is: where should we be starting from? What are the participants bringing to this situation in terms of their (life and/or ministry) experience, their prior knowledge and their expectations? Or, to put it more simply, what difference will it make?

Different approaches

James Hopewell (1987) proposes four models used by those seeking to join a church (using house-hunting as an analogy): contextual, mechanistic, organic and symbolic. He suggests that house-hunters and church-seekers have a dominant theme when considering a new house or new church (although each of the four perspectives will play a part). So, the contextual seeker will be focused on local environment and context, the mechanistic on functionality, the organic on the future possibilities and the symbolic on what the choice will say of them to the world.

It is a very useful model for those engaging (or potentially engaging) in any form of ministry or Christian development. The four approaches can be readily identified (although I must emphasize that the approaches are not mutually exclusive, but rather suggest a dominant theme). There will be those who seek development primarily because of the context and environment in which it sits, choosing those elements which particularly suit the landscape of their life or ministry – and perhaps because it fits comfortably with the landscape in which they are situated: the contextual seekers. Then there will be those who seek development opportunities primarily as a result of identifying specific needs in ministry or their Christian journey. They need a new skill or have a particular question or area of concern which they require addressing: the mechanistic seekers. Third, there will be those who undertake development primarily to discover new possibilities in ministry or in their lives, to open new doors and to find out what it is that they don't know, to help them grow organically. Finally, there will be those who will undertake development primarily in order to say something about themselves, anything from showing the vicar or bishop that they are jumping through a particular hoop to having a course or qualification on their CV: the symbolic seeker.

Not only are these dominant starting points not mutually exclusive – seekers are likely to have mixed motives, which can change during the experience of undertaking a particular piece of development – neither are they necessarily predominant in a particular person or personality. Different stages in life, different life experiences and different ministries and ministry situations are all likely to influence the dominant theme adopted by an individual.

Perhaps the most important lesson for those providing a development opportunity is awareness of potential participants' mixed motives. When providing such opportunities a variety of approaches will always need to be adopted, a theme I will return to.

Importantly, though, for those providing development opportunities there will almost inevitably be a tendency to adopt either the mechanistic or the organic approach. It would actually be much less easy – though not impossible – to adopt either the contextual or symbolic approach, as the contextual approach will tend to be far too specific to an individual's own situation and the symbolic approach to an individual's personal needs.

An organic approach

In any given situation the temptation will be to choose a mechanistic approach to development, for one very simple reason. Whether I'm a trainer of clergy or a parish priest, a bishop or a consultant brought in to do some training, I will believe that I have a fairly clear understanding of what the organization (diocese, parish, small group) needs. The issue will be, therefore: how do I best get my message across? How do I train this bunch of people to be better leaders, to grasp better the basics of baptism, to have a better understanding of St John's Gospel?

The task seems to be clear; the issue is, how do I best fulfil the given task? It seems a simple 'from point A to point B' formula. But what this approach loses is the baggage, the history, the personalities, the needs that any participant brings to the given situation.

A simple example – and huge learning point for me – was the yearly round of annual parochial church meetings as a vicar. Each year we would go through the grind of persuading (or dissuading!) people to stand for election as churchwardens and to the Parochial Church Council (PCC). We had a certain number of places to fill so we had to find people to fill them.

It gradually dawned on me that it wouldn't be the end of the world if the vacancies were not filled, and rather than asking how I should fill these spaces the better question was, 'How do I help develop in appropriate roles the people God has sent to this church?' Rather than cramming roundish pegs into fairly square holes, I began to think along the lines of 'Here are some round pegs: how can I hone the holes so that there is a good fit?' We began to develop ministries which suited the skills and talents that people brought, rather than doing stuff because 'that's what churches do'.

This process in turn challenged me to look at the way that PCCs were run. For those who were prepared to sit on PCCs, was the way that we ran the PCC making the best use of their time, their talents and their energy – or were we running a meeting because we've always done it this way? Transforming the meeting not only raised the energy levels but also gradually had an effect on those who were prepared to stand for election. And the amazing reality was that by using this organic approach not only did we get as much work done (usually in a shorter period) but we also had people who were more fulfilled in their ministry.

Ultimately, people began to see that they were being fulfilled in ministry, and the very clear side effect was that God's Church increasingly became a place of mission, growing accordingly. In common parlance, people discovered that there was something in it for them (and then for others, because they brought their friends).

I developed this approach in my work with clergy training and development when introducing a Work and Ministry Consultancy Scheme for clergy. I was aware that in some parishes there were a number of people who worked in the area of management consultancy, human relations, etc., and had considerable skills which could assist clergy in their ministry. I therefore advertised for such people to offer their services, undertook an interview process, and appointed some (though not all) of the applicants – to offer their services for free!

Those appointed were delighted, first, to be taken seriously and approached professionally and, second, to be offering back something to the Church, in a real spirit of stewardship, which they felt fully equipped to do (rather than being squeezed into a vacancy on their local PCC).

The consultants worked (and continue to work) with clergy who wished to avail themselves of this ministry and I expected each to draw up a clear contract and understanding on which the arrangement was to be based. The whole scheme works fully organically, and I will not take clergy who are 'referred by their bishop', etc., but only those who themselves want to develop their ministry (often identified in their annual ministerial development review).

My experience, then, strongly suggests that an organic approach to development is likely to be most fruitful, because it addresses the issues that are of concern to individuals, rather than stemming from organizational need. It meant that the organization had to adapt accordingly, but not as much as might have been thought.

This approach was supported by some research[1] that I undertook with recently retired diocesan bishops, exploring their experience and attitudes towards continuing professional development (CPD), both for themselves and as policy makers for the Church of England and implementers in their own dioceses. All the bishops, while emphasizing the importance of an organized approach to continuing professional development, regarded the imposition of mandatory CPD (which would be a mechanistic approach) to be both undesirable and unworkable. Among the reasons given included the vastly differing situations in which clergy minister, the difficulty in policing such a system, the nature of the ministry to which clergy are called, the underlying culture of both Church and the clerical profession, and the clear benefits of providing high-quality CPD which was attractive enough for clergy to want to participate, rather than clergy feeling they were being cajoled into participating against their will. All of these themes I shall be returning to later in this book.

The organic approach, then, at its heart addresses the basic human question, 'What's in it for me?' However, it sees this not as a selfish, individually centred context, but rather in the context of a Church whose purpose is to proclaim by word and works the good news of Jesus Christ. So perhaps this is better expressed as, 'What's in it for me as an individual, made in the image and likeness of God, called to a community of faith, as a follower of Jesus Christ?'

Developing themes

In this book I shall explore this organic approach to Christian development with reference to a number of themes:

- starting where people are, as individuals, groups and congregations
- acknowledging and addressing inherited culture and expectations
- developing complementary approaches
- exploring individual needs, skills and preferences
- ensuring appropriate review and reflection
- integrating a collaborative and co-operative approach
- being organized and responsive.

So, in the next chapter I shall develop the importance of beginning any training and development agenda with the individuals concerned, the local church and the local situation. I will discuss the issue of why so many grand initiatives and over-structured approaches seem to fail.

In Chapter 3 I explore the importance of inherited culture, amplifying the imperative of taking received culture seriously and seeing the context as it really is, not as we would like it to be. I will then show how and why appropriate ministry development can be a major factor in culture change.

Chapter 4 offers reflections on complementary approaches. I demonstrate how any good ministry development will include a rich mix of skills training, theological education and personal and spiritual formation. In unpacking the difference between these three headlines I will show why all three need to be present in an appropriate mix for fruitful development.

Chapter 5 returns to the theme of context and focuses on the importance of individual identity and personal needs and preferences while developing in Christian ministry. I also address the key place of vocational discernment, calling and selection when considering major areas of Christian development. The nature of the ministry context and the matching of the needs of the context to individual calling and vocation will be a major theme of this chapter.

It is crucial to acknowledge that needs and situations change; just because something works once doesn't mean that it will work every time. And if something didn't work, why didn't it work? Chapter 6 therefore addresses the need for regular reflection and review. While proposing that both formal and informal processes for reflection and review should always be a part of any Christian development, I will also discuss the central place of ministerial development review (MDR) for both ordained and lay ministers (and what 'good MDR' looks like).

Chapter 7 reminds us that, in the words of John Donne, 'No man is an island.' Here is the emphasis that ministry is not a lone endeavour, but that all are God's ministers, working in co-operation with the Holy Spirit and in collaboration with other ministers and with the whole people of God. Although we might well start with the 'What's in it for me?' question, this is only appropriate if seen within the wider context of building community within the love of God. Underlining the whole endeavour, then, is a 'Trinitarian' and relational approach to ministry.

In Chapter 8 I will offer an organized, yet open, approach to training and development which includes seven practical steps. These, I suggest, if taken seriously and proportionally, will give an appropriately structural underpinning for effective and fruitful ministry development.

Coda

The *Oxford English Dictionary* describes the word 'organic' in this context as meaning 'characterized by or designating continuous or natural development'. So much in the Gospels points towards Jesus working with the raw material, the expectations, that are presented. Whether it's the parable of the sower, which recognizes the importance of the context in which the sower sows, or the people Jesus encounters and surrounds himself with – a tax collector, fishermen, a Zealot – Jesus' life reflects an organic approach to his ministry and mission. Jesus' earthly ministry is characterized by the continual and natural development of people among whom he spends his time; he never expects them to be other than the people they are, yet he helps to develop them to play their part in the spreading of the good news.

2

Whose agenda?

> Interpretation lies at the heart of wisdom, for in its many mani-
> festations, wisdom is always a way of looking at reality that finds
> patterns, connections and meanings . . . biblical wisdom is shot
> through with the vocabulary and imagery of 'seeing'. Having
> 'insight', 'perception' or 'illumination' are among the gifts that
> characterize the wise.
>
> (Michael Sadgrove, *Wisdom and Ministry*)[1]

Following a particularly frustrating PCC meeting, when nobody
really seemed to get the importance of the subject I had introduced for discussion, a very wise and experienced priest gently
reminded me of one simple fact which put the whole matter
into context. Remember, he said, being vicar of this parish takes
up the largest part of your waking hours. For everyone else on
the PCC, the parish takes up no more than a few hours each
week, with work, family and so many other concerns coming
before the business of running a church. Their priorities will
never be your priorities, however hard you try.

This was a piece of advice I was later able to apply in reverse
when the latest diocesan initiative came down from on high
(as I then perceived it). Once I had recovered my anger that
the bishop had failed (in my eyes) to realize that I was working
my socks off already without another grand plan to implement,
I reflected on my friend's wisdom. The bishop's agenda was not
my agenda; his immediate priorities were not mine.

Now being one of those perceived to be 'on high', as Director
of Ministry, I am concerned not to impose my agenda on others.
The highest priority in laying on any training and development

will be that it is worthwhile for those participating and not a way of simply giving clergy, parishioners or staff more work to do or imposing yet more guilt.

The question of 'Whose agenda is this serving?' can act as a simple litmus test for any training and development we might put on. In this chapter I will explore a number of situations in which training and development is provided and encouraged in a church environment, considering how appropriate agendas can be met and how participation can be enriching.

Continuing ministerial development

As I write this, new clergy terms and conditions of service are being put in place in the Church of England. One of the provisions of these terms and conditions is an expectation that clergy will engage in continuing professional development (CPD) or life-long learning throughout their ministry. The clear implication is that this should be agreed and quantifiable, and that records should be kept. In principle I have no argument with this, but in practice I fear that it is a very dangerous 'rule' to set. It offers a licence for box-ticking and hurdle-jumping; in other words, it can end up as clergy having to prove that they have attended a certain number of CPD days each year so that a box can be ticked on their record.

Continuing professional development (or, in Church of England language, continuing ministerial development, CMD) is, I believe, crucial in today's rapidly changing world, not just for clergy but for all engaged in any professional work and in all ministry endeavours. But – and this is a huge but – it should never become a box-ticking exercise.

When I was a vicar in west London one of the churchwardens, a solicitor, arrived at an evening meeting looking wrung out. As a single-handed practitioner it was necessary for her to attend two CPD events annually to maintain her practising certificate. It transpired that in order to fulfil this requirement she had paid a great deal of money to be crammed into a lecture hall with 2,000 other solicitors for the best part of ten hours and was talked at by a series of speakers. From her description there was no attempt at presentation which gave appropriate adult education, the environment was highly inappropriate, and she felt that no effective learning had taken place during the day. However, she could tick the box! She was very cross and depressed by the whole experience, and described those who put on the day as 'having a licence to make money'. Her telling me this story was, in part, my inspiration for engaging in this work, and (as a practising clergy development officer) led me to take a step back and look at the CPD that I was presenting and facilitating.

There are times when I would wish for some sort of compulsion to get clergy to attend CPD events, but this story always acts, for me, as a cautionary tale of how 'proven CPD as a condition of continued licensing' can easily give space for unfocused and poorly presented events, and for clergy feeling that professional development is solely about 'jumping through hoops'. In some professions CPD has spawned a whole industry, and the quality of some of what is on offer is highly dubious.

So, a key question for an appropriate model for CPD is, 'Whose agenda?' Is CPD about proving that clergy are professionals like other professions and have ticked boxes, or is it about encouraging clergy to cultivate the habit of continuous and life-long learning and development to support and develop them in their ministry?

If the latter (which clearly I believe it is), those providing and encouraging clergy to engage in CPD will need to be clear that what is being offered responds to the needs of clergy, of the Church and of the imperatives of the gospel, in an environment which is conducive to good learning. It needs to be presented in such a way that the participants don't feel they're there simply because they have to be, because it ticks the appropriate box.

I believe this indicates, then, that mandatory CMD offers a mechanistic approach, with a clear tendency to serve the (perceived) needs of the institution rather than the individual and his or her situation. In order to ensure that CMD is both fruitful and relevant, an organic approach will be essential. In this context an organic approach will take into account a number of key features.

Clergy character

It is important to pay attention to the sort of people who become clergy. By the nature of their role and ministry, clergy will tend to be self-starters who are not easily line-managed. Clergy ministry is multi-faceted; priests and pastors are expected to be leaders in mission and ministry in their parish. They will often best be 'entrepreneurs', working with parishes and congregations to discover and implement the particular vision of the Church that God is calling them to in their given situation.

Clergy ministry, then, tends to militate strongly against compliance with organizational structural imperatives. Generally speaking, most clergy will respond to the specific authority of their bishop (even though such authority is hard to substantiate in tangible outcomes), but structural authority and compulsion will tend to be rejected as inappropriate and meaningless by the majority.

Quality

If, then, I believe that compulsion is not an appropriate method by which to engender engagement in professional development, one of the principal ways that clergy will be encouraged (or discouraged) to take CMD seriously is by the quality of what is on offer. Those involved in providing and encouraging CMD in a diocese will be (appropriately) challenged to provide training and development of a high quality, which is well focused to the needs of participants.

The aim will always be that clergy will engage with continuing professional development because it's a worthwhile thing to do and not because they're told to. Bishops, archdeacons and those with responsibility for clergy development will serve clergy far better as encouragers than as enforcers. As one bishop put it, 'Ultimately I can't make clergy do anything, but I can woo them.'

Culture

The Church has in the past had an unfortunate association with things being done shoddily and without proper care and attention. I often think that church kitchens can be symbolic of this; are the cupboards full of non-matching cups and saucers that people were going to throw away but have given to the church instead, or that have been rescued from jumble sales – the 'I didn't want it any more so I thought I'd give it to the church' syndrome? Or is decent tea and coffee served in good-quality mugs or cups such as I would be proud to have in my own home? My attitude as a vicar was always, 'If it's not good enough for your home then it's certainly not good enough for God's church.'

This axiom is utterly transferable to the quality of training and development; it should be appropriately professional. This does not necessarily mean spending lots of money on glossy brochures, but rather is concerned with the approach and attitude with which it is presented; this is a vital theme to which I shall be returning in Chapter 8.

An appropriately professional and organic approach to CMD, therefore, will return huge benefit. In modelling good practice, treating clergy like professional adults and using occasions to demonstrate a supporting and developing milieu, those responsible in a diocese can predicate culture change. I shall develop this notion further in the next chapter.

Affirmation and accountability

An excellent report was produced in 2002 by the Society of Mary and Martha, entitled *Affirmation and Accountability* (Lee and Horsman 2002). The essence of its findings was that clergy generally lacked affirmation in their role but also failed to see themselves as accountable. The report called on church leaders to address these fundamental issues which contributed to negativity and breakdown among clergy.

Both of these issues are entirely apposite in any discussion on clergy CMD. On the one hand, if clergy fail to see themselves as accountable in any way (either to their local congregations and ministry situations or to their bishops and colleagues) there will be little incentive to engage in continuing development and to see themselves as part of a learning and developing community.

Conversely, engagement in a wide variety of forms of professional development will present individuals with excellent opportunities to find affirmation and support in their roles, which will be enhanced through engaging with colleagues.

Good-quality and appropriately professional CPD will assist clergy in feeling accountable to their bishops and colleagues particularly, but also by extension to their ministry situations in the way that such CPD is applied. Such CPD, though, when well organized and delivered will also be supportive and challenging, both through the content and through the context of delivery.

Contextual

Clearly it will not be possible to have an individual programme developed with each member of the clergy in mind, but it will be important to bear the varied local contexts in mind, offering at the very least an understanding that parishes vary hugely in terms of church tradition, demography, expectations, challenges and so much more. Sweeping statements and attitudes, suggesting a one-size-fits-all approach, will inevitably be alienating.

Wherever possible, though, local and individual contexts will be taken into account, as not only will participants feel valued in recognizing themselves and their contexts in discussions, but huge dividends will be gleaned in terms of ownership of the learning process. A simple example of this can be to get participants to share something of their own story in terms of CPD and to discuss how the learning or skills might be applied by them to their local situation.

Walter Wink (1990), for example, suggests that every Bible study should begin by simply asking each participant to share one thing that strikes him or her about the passage under discussion today. This is received by the leader, and thence by the group, without comment but appreciatively, whatever that thought is. The immediate effect is that everyone has buy-in to the Bible study.

The dangers of a mechanistic approach

The danger, then, of a mechanistic approach to CPD is the tendency of identifying 'what's wrong' (with the Church, the clergy, the institutions, etc.) and then proposing a line of CPD for clergy to remedy the situation. A current example of this is the area of leadership. It has become self-evident that good and appropriate leadership in parish ministry is a key to growth and development. The converse also seems to be true, that very often where parishes are withering and declining a major factor can be the lack of good leadership.

Some very good clergy leadership programmes have now been developed both within dioceses and by other organizations (the CPAS Arrow Course for young church leaders[2] being an exceptional example). However, in some situations this cause-and-effect relationship has been met with a straight response of 'We must get all our clergy trained in leadership.' A number of dioceses proudly proclaim that all – or large percentages of – their stipendiary clergy have now undertaken their diocesan leadership course. It certainly looks good on paper, but I do wonder what real effect this has had on their ministries and on the mission of the Church. If it's presented in such a way that clergy feel they have to comply by attending a particular piece of training or event, then ultimately the majority will do so;

but there will be a real question in my mind as to what extent they will be partaking in a co-operative venture.

My experience has, rather, been to offer courses, residentials and opportunities that participants are keen to take part in because the word is out that this is worth doing. If I am struggling to get participants, then I will soon be questioning whether what I'm offering is appropriate. Simply getting people through a leadership programme will never improve their leadership skills and ability. It is much more about engaging with people and their issues where they find themselves, and engaging them in a process of discovery and change. This is an issue which we will continue to explore throughout this book.

Parish pastoral visiting team

One of the realities of parish life and ministry today is that there can no longer be an expectation that the vicar will be the person to carry out all pastoral ministry in a parish. In simple practical terms, with the increased complexities and pressure on an incumbent today and the diverse and complex lives that people lead, it is simply not credible to expect one person to carry out all the pastoral visiting and care once associated with clergy ministry – whether or not this is seen as appropriate.

With this in mind, many parishes will explore the need to develop a scheme or to train or encourage individual members to carry out pastoral ministry on behalf of the church. Many dioceses will have off-the-peg courses to train pastoral assistants on behalf of parishes and there will also be schemes to train teams in their local setting. All of this is highly commendable, but I wonder how much of such schemes and training is meeting need, and really exploring whether individual skills, interests and development are being taken into account. In short, is this a mechanistic approach to solving a problem, or is there an attempt to address the issues organically?

Expedient or theologically appropriate?

The first mechanistic assumption that I would suggest needs unpacking is the underlying reason for developing lay involvement in pastoral ministry. In my introduction to this section I presented the assumption that the increase in lay involvement was simply due to the fact that the vicar no longer had time to carry out such ministry and that there aren't as many clergy as there used to be. An organic approach, however, would make no such assumption. Rather than beginning with expediency – with who can 'help the vicar' – I would suggest the starting point should be the theological basis for such an approach to ministry.

In returning to first principles, in asking the 'why' rather than the 'how', there is a much greater likelihood of developing a ministry which is both owned and understood by the parish.

In developing a pastoral ministry team while a vicar in a parish, I began by writing a Lent study course which explored the theological background to the Church's commitment to pastoral ministry (a copy of the Lent course can be found at the back of the book, in Appendix 1). Over a number of weeks several groups around the parish looked at a number of aspects and expressions of the Church's care and concern for community and the individuals within it. The course concluded by asking participants what they considered an appropriate response for the parish should be. Out of the response the concept of a parish visiting team was born.

Then, and only then, did I invite the PCC to consider the possibility of inviting individuals to a training course to become a pastoral visiting team. By this stage there were also sufficient people on the PCC who had a real understanding of what such a scheme might offer. The concept had grown organically.

To visit and care for whom?

A visiting or pastoral care team is a grand scheme and once worked through both practically and theologically can be seen to be exactly what a good parish church should be about; it's hardly controversial! However, the issue then has to be faced as to who is to be cared for or visited. The simple answer would seem to be whoever the vicar passes on. However, such a solution has two basic mechanistic-orientated problems: first, it returns to being a problem-solving scheme and second, it means that the team are merely an appendage of the vicar, dependent upon the incumbent remembering to pass names to the team. Both a philosophical and a practical problem are presented; the team are still effectively the vicar's helpers.

The clear solution to this is to involve the team in developing a pastoral care policy for the parish. The simplest and most effective way of doing this is to include it within the training programme, so that towards the end of such a programme a session (which necessarily includes the incumbent) will be dedicated to developing a clear policy of who is to be cared for and by whom, and how this is to be undertaken. This policy can then be discussed and agreed by the PCC.

Again, this is an organic solution to the nature of pastoral ministry in the parish, which gives maximum ownership both to the team and to the incumbent, and which will not be dependent upon the incumbent. The policy will have developed with wide involvement and can be widely promulgated but can be really very simple (this should certainly not be bureaucratic in nature).

The team, for example, might be dedicated to baptism and funeral visiting; to electoral roll visiting (ensuring that all regular members of the congregation are cared for); to visiting the elderly and housebound; to visiting those referred by outside agencies (e.g. doctors' surgeries, Age Concern and social services); or to responding to need.

The organic process will have identified the particular issues of the parish and the skills, numbers and availability of individuals, and how this all fits together with the theological understandings that have been explored and agreed.

Fundraising

Fundraising might not immediately seem a good example to feature here, but I am passionate about addressing this particular issue appropriately, as it is one which most parishes will face one way or another periodically. The usual approach to fundraising in my experience is: here is a problem or challenge, how do we raise the money? It then becomes an issue concerning the best way to dress it up attractively – a simple mechanistic approach. An organic approach to the issue will not only make the task much more interesting and engaging but will, I believe, ensure that fundraising is placed firmly as a mission activity.

The place to start any fundraising or financial issue facing a church is not the balance sheet but the Bible. As stewardship advisers love to remind us, Jesus has more to say on money than on any other subject. But I would actually take the issue one step further back in exploring it theologically. Laurie Green (2009) reminds us that any issue, and any given situation, can be explored from a contextual or theological standpoint. Certainly my experience of applying Green's principles in an inner-city parish where I was vicar paid huge dividends.

By beginning not with 'How do we raise some ridiculous sum of money because the church is falling down?' but rather with the theological question of 'What is our church?', we certainly began a major fundraising endeavour on a much more optimistic basis. Importantly, though, it was not just optimism that gave us a firm foundation in the project, but an organic approach to the whole issue.

In involving a small group initially, and then a wide constituency in the congregation, in reflecting and exploring theologically we engaged people with the 'why' question long before we got to the 'how'. The project was owned and seen as something belonging locally.

Later I was to work with professional fundraisers[3] in another parish, but their message, although not strictly theological, was similar. They talked of their business being about organized common sense and of addressing the basic questions of ownership before any issue of getting the money in.

Twelve disciples

It is, of course, no coincidence that Jesus chose 12 disciples. Social psychologists and those involved in group dynamics constantly tell us that the size of a small group is crucial to its life and vitality. Numbers from seven to 16 are frequently cited as being a good size for effective group dynamics, depending upon the situation and leadership.

One of the things I will frequently suggest to new incumbents is that they develop a small group of around 12 people in the parish to accompany them, in some way, during the early stages of their ministry. The PCC is an essential part of parish life, but it is at its heart a mechanistic body. It has a clear function or functions and its very existence depends upon given criteria. Although it can be developed organically, there are in-built limitations.

The group of 12 I suggest will be completely separate from the committee structure (though may well include some of the same people). It will need some sort of a hook to give it a *raison d'être*, but almost anything will do. Perhaps it's a Bible study group meeting in the vicarage or a Growing Leaders[4] group, or it may be an envisioning group. It may (as with one vicar I know) develop out of another group – in his case a stewardship working party. The important thing is that it has a fairly open brief and will include people who can wrestle with issues and listen to one another.

The place of this group will be to model organic development for the parish, to open up possibilities and to develop potential for leadership. The incumbent's role will be on the one hand to offer informal training in discipleship and on the other to listen attentively to what is happening beneath the surface in the parish.

It will never be possible to get a truly representative group of people, but a good selection of people from the parish will be useful. The issue of this group being seen as a clique or as the vicar's 'club' will need to be carefully handled, but is not insurmountable.

Establishing, using and, importantly, learning from this group will pay dividends for future ministry in the parish. It will also model good practice and begin to identify future leaders. Drawing on people from the fringe will also help people to feel included, as well as widening the catchment for future ministry.

Lent groups and house groups

My final example will not endear me to the publishing industry! However, so often the response to the approach of Lent by a busy parish priest is a scramble to (1) persuade people to join groups and (2) find some suitable material. Lent groups are what we do during Lent so (mechanistically) how do we make them happen?

The organic response is, I believe, painfully simple – though painful is the operative word. The vicar, or another competent person in the parish, should consider writing it him- or herself. So often, Lent group material is 'very interesting' but can be of no real relevance or application to individuals and their local situation. Locally written material can address the real questions that are confronting people, asking good, open questions for discussion. (See Appendix 1.)

Lent group material, I would suggest, does not need to be carefully crafted prose, but simply some good relevant material which opens discussion. It will then be up to small-group leaders (who will have received some appropriate training) to keep discussion on track and flowing.

The benefit of this approach will not only be that the annual scramble for material will be averted, but more importantly the word will get out that such groups are worth coming to:

they're not just an intellectual exercise, but they are about me and my discipleship.

I have used the example of Lent groups, but I would strongly suggest that the model is transferable to house groups and to other issues of Christian discipleship.

One of the issues that I am confronted with over and over again by clergy is the difficulty in engaging congregation members in effective Christian discipleship. By approaching this issue organically rather than mechanistically, by growing the issue at a local level rather than imposing a model from outside, I would suggest that people will begin to see that it is more vital to their own lives. Material does not necessarily need to be developed by one person but can itself be raised up through a dynamic process.

Busy clergy will, I'm sure, ask, 'When exactly am I supposed to spend time doing this in my schedule?' It is my conjecture that this work of developing Christian disciples is at the heart of priestly ministry and can certainly be seen alongside preaching as being an essential part of the teaching ministry to which we are ordained. Developing and honing the skills required will pay huge dividends (or, of course, where appropriate, co-opting the skills of Readers, Licensed Lay Ministers, other lay theologians, teachers or writers).

Incidentally, I am not for a moment dismissing the use of carefully prepared and well-tested published material. It is both/and, not either/or.

Conclusion

Our Christian faith is, at its heart, relational. In reading the Gospels we see Jesus' teaching in the context of his relationships. In asking, 'Whose agenda?' I am asking a question of relationships, as the organic approach to Christian development is fundamentally about relationships. John Adair (1987) in his model of 'action-centred leadership' talks of a good leader

juggling the three facets of task, individual and group mainten-
ance needs; he is clear that a good leader will need to balance
all three aspects. To interpret for this context, in order to achieve
any task the relational elements of both individual and group
needs and ownership are crucial. An organic approach will
ensure that individual and group agendas are being addressed
(even if not fully met) in order that a task may be approached
appropriately.

3

Working below the surface

Growth is the only evidence of life.

(John Henry Newman)[1]

Every parish, every diocese, every ministry situation has a unique culture. It may look similar to the church up the road or the diocese next door, but it will be unique, having developed over years or generations. The culture will vary with changes in leadership, but to undertake major culture change is a mammoth task which certainly can happen (I have witnessed culture being transformed in the diocese in which I have ministered for over 25 years), but does not happen easily or without clarity, appropriate leadership, wrestling and pain.

To recognize that each ministry situation is unique may, on the one hand, seem basic common sense (which of course it is). On the other hand, though, I would suggest that in developing ministry this recognition is a vital ingredient in the mix. It is never possible to use a model of ministry development in two different situations in exactly the same way. Not only do the individuals concerned vary, but the culture of which they are a part will be different and will have a significant impact on the work in hand.

The first two parishes in which I ministered after ordination were in the East End of London – in Tower Hamlets and then Hackney. Having worked in the Health Service in Tower Hamlets prior to ordination, I guess that by the time I moved on to be an incumbent in Hackney I felt I was beginning to understand what the issues were and something about working in the inner city. I confess that it was quite a long time into a ten-year incumbency before I realized that I was having to unlearn and re-learn. Each situation is different, even if many of the characteristics are similar.

This reality was brought home to me forcibly when I was invited to work with my neighbouring parishes on a local lay development programme. Our church found a number of candidates and we embraced the programme enthusiastically. I was then a little bemused to discover that there were no candidates from my neighbouring parish – a parish with a congregational profile very similar to our own. When I discussed this with the vicar (with whom I got on well), I was astonished to hear him say that there wasn't anyone suitable in the congregation: 'People don't do that sort of thing at this church.'

It was easy to plant the familiar accusation at his door, that as vicar he was 'blocking' the development of the laity. However, on closer examination I discovered that the situation was far more complex than this. The culture of this church, it seemed to me, militated against lay leadership and lay involvement, and this culture traced its roots back over many generations and many incumbencies. The prevailing culture seemed to suggest collusion between vicar and people over clericalism and lay passivity. Conversely, the inherited culture at the church where I was vicar had bred lay leadership and enablement.

I often wonder in parishes where history repeats itself with a new incumbent whether the parish has managed to attract a 'vicar-like-us' or whether the incumbent has 'gone native' because culture change has proved too difficult or perhaps the reality of culture has not been fully identified.

In this chapter I would like to suggest, therefore, that identifying culture and making active decisions as to which particular aspects of prevailing culture need to be – and can be – changed, which aspects need to be worked with and/or lived with, and which aspects it is simply not worth bothering with, is crucial to the whole business of developing ministry.

Many years ago my work and ministry consultant – a priest who had just retired from a senior position in the Church of England – said to me that every church has its sticking points, and sometimes it's just not worth challenging them but rather finding a way of working around them. At the same church in Hackney I realized early on that I could introduce any number of new hymns and songs at the Parish Eucharist as long as I left the Anglican chant psalm between the readings alone! At the time it just didn't seem worth the aggravation of changing this particular element, especially when there were other clear ways of rejuvenating worship.

Being clear about the prevailing culture and making active, positive decisions as to how to deal with each aspect of it will set a very firm foundation in which ministry can be developed. It may be that the operative culture is one that actively welcomes development and the changes and adjustments that are required to refresh ministry, but this condition is rare. Human institutions and groups have an innate tendency to resist change. In science this tendency is called homeostasis; as the dictionary says, 'a tendency to reach equilibrium, either metabolically within a cell or organism or socially and psychologically within an individual or group'. Or, to put it another way, we're quite happy where we are, and whatever you do we'll find a way of restoring our natural equilibrium.

I suggest, therefore, that it is not about whether or not there is a natural culture which promotes development and growth, but rather at what point resistance will take place and what it will be within the culture that will militate against development. Managing change in order to promote (or further promote) a culture of development in ministry will be a necessary tool in the toolkit. In this chapter, then, I shall explore how we identify prevailing culture in the context of managing change. Having done this, I will then go on to look at how and why appropriate ministry development can be a major factor in changing a whole culture.

Managing change

In implementing effective change which will fruitfully engender a culture of development there are four significant factors which need to be taken into account, illustrated in Figure 1.

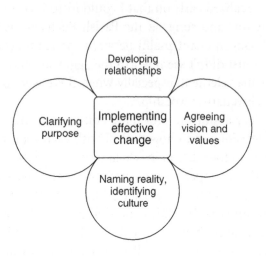

Figure 1

None of these four elements predominates and there is no necessary sequence (various of the elements can take place at the same time), but I am convinced that for effective change to take place each element must be taken seriously. Further, though, I would maintain that promoting and developing a culture of ministry and Christian development will create a foundation for other necessary culture change, and it will provide an environment for partnership in living the good news of Jesus Christ, of individual and corporate ownership of the gospel.

Developing relationships

The gospel is at its heart relational. Jesus was born into an earthly family; he carried out his ministry among the communities of first-century Palestine; he called disciples to share in his ministries and travelling. But more than this, the whole Bible is concerned with the interweaving of relationships in communities and of course with the growing and developing relationship between God and God's people.

And in our Christian faith we take this one stage further by placing God as Trinity at the centre of our faith. We believe and trust in God, who reveals God's self as Father, Son and Spirit; Creator, Redeemer and Sustainer: a God who is in relationship with God's self. As Christians we are called to be in relationship with our fellow Christians and with our neighbours. It is through these relationships that we act out our Christian lives.

So it is that in relationships we build communities and build trust. In order to establish a culture of development it will be essential that we know something of one another's lives and stories, as developing in Christian ministry cannot take place in a vacuum but rather in the context of individuals' whole lives. In developing relationships we develop the context in which a culture of development can find firm foundations.

I will return to this theme in Chapter 7, but suffice to say at this stage that any attempt to effect change without a community of maturing relationships will founder on lack of trust and depth of understanding, however strong the vision appears to be.[2]

Agreeing vision and values

Why is it that, over and again these days, interviewees for the role of incumbent in a parish are asked the question, 'What is your vision for ministry in this parish?' or some similar question? The answer must surely be, 'I don't have one!' Unless, of course, it is broad generalities like, 'To serve the needs of the gospel' or 'To grow disciples of Jesus' – great lines, but pretty abstract.

I am highly suspicious of any model of priestly ministry or Christian leadership which arrives with a ready-made vision. Jesus spent 30 years living in his community before he stood up in the synagogue and declared his vision (Luke 4.16–21). I am also, incidentally, highly suspicious of the model of ministry which says (as I did), 'I'm not going to change anything in my first year: I simply want to listen and observe.' This, as I quickly discovered, is ludicrous, as my presence as the new vicar, doing things in the way I did them, without realizing, was a change and effected change. In the opening months of a new ministry what is required is honesty and openness; I am not my predecessor.

Vision, I am convinced, is something which needs to be developed corporately and co-operatively. Certainly the incumbent, the bishop, the senior pastor will be a key person in the process of developing vision, as will other leaders and ministers. A vision which is presented ready formed will never be owned, but one which is collected and shaped will belong to everyone and will form the DNA of the culture of a church, or any other organization for that matter.

The first step will be to agree the values; this will be a very specific exercise allowing open contribution and not just saying, 'We agree gospel values.' It should give examples and should describe who we think we are and what we think we're about as a community.

Once a clear picture of who we think we are and what we think we are about has been established, the next stage will be to develop a vision. This will include hopes and aspirations along with priorities and practical steps in carrying out the vision. In developing both values and vision there should be maximum participation from the whole community; the more people involved in the process – even marginally involved – the more ownership will take place.

Agreeing and establishing a clear set of values for a community and articulating an agreed vision will be a major contribution to transforming culture. However, the mistake is to think that just because we have a vision, and even if every member of the community can express that vision, we have established a new culture.

For example, a church may go through a values exercise which establishes that one of its key aspirational values is to place a wide range of lay ministries at the heart of the church. It may then work hard at producing a vision which sets a variety of lay leadership and ministerial roles as a priority. The church next works to produce a Mission Action Plan which names the ministries, setting SMART[3] goals towards this end. The church community has been made aware of the wealth of research which points towards the clear evidence that a broad-based lay leadership and well-trained and established lay ministries will be a major contributor to church growth,[4] yet it seems that, despite best endeavours, nothing is moving. There may even be people willing and able to undertake the leadership and ministry roles, but there seems to be an intangible blockage. What's gone wrong?

So, a crucial part of the process of effective and fruitful change is a reality check.

Naming reality, identifying culture

As discussed earlier, all human institutions and groups have an innate tendency to resist change, and God's Church is no exception! Whenever change is proposed there will naturally be four attitudes or positions at work. In order to work with change it will be crucial to identify each (and of course there will be shades of each rather than absolutes). The four sets of attitudes or positioning can be characterized as in Figure 2 overleaf.

I suggest that each member of the community, organization or institution where change is proposed will take up one of these four positions, whether consciously or unconsciously. And for those involved in managing change it will be crucial to name this reality at an early stage, and to keep a constant check on this as the change process progresses. Those who resist change and those who engage with change are usually the easiest to cope with, because at least you know where they stand (although this can be more complex than it seems, as we shall

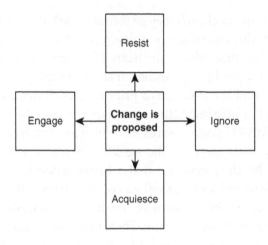

Figure 2

go on to see). The more difficult are those who simply ignore change and pretend it's not happening and those who are taking the easy way of acquiescing without engaging.

Resist

Those who resist change are, ironically, probably the easiest group to deal with as they are likely to be vocal or at least clear in their resistance. With those who resist, it will be important to clarify what their objections are and explore whether there are ways in which concessions can be made to help them to become more amenable to change. However, their resistance may well be nebulous ('we've always done it this way'), based on loyalty to the previous vicar or to others who are also resisting or, more bluntly, because they don't like change.

A great danger will be to spend too much time listening to this group and/or making concessions which so water down the proposed change that it becomes unworkable.

Ignore

On the surface, those who ignore change might seem quite easy to deal with – we simply ignore them! However, it is never likely to be that simple. Take the classic example, which occurred many times in the 1960s and 1970s, of the one old man or woman left in a house as a slum clearance programme was taking place. Each time the person concerned became a *cause célèbre* by doing nothing. To remove the person the authorities would be seen as cruel and heartless, but by ignoring what was going on around him or her they were holding up a whole development.

Ignoring can really be very close to resisting (a form of passive resistance) but is much harder to deal with as the person concerned cannot be reasoned with. This person's attitude can be characterized as 'This has nothing to do with me; I am simply not interested.' Yet the reality of passive resistance is that it works insidiously by creating an atmosphere of passive aggression which can sour a whole community.

Sometimes, of course, ignoring is a genuine standpoint of really believing that 'this has nothing to do with me'. Anyone who has given out the notices during a church service will be aware of this sort of ignoring! Whether it's an appeal for help for a working party, a stewardship campaign, an appeal for children's work leaders or an invitation to a church social, there is almost always a general feeling around the church that 'this has nothing to do with me'.

In this situation it is much more about finding different and imaginative ways of presenting information and inviting a response. As I shall discuss later, nothing beats a personal, individualized invitation as a way of involving people in a new venture.

Acquiesce

It is my firm opinion, based on painful experience, that acquiescence is the most difficult attitude to counter. I have lost count of the number of PCC meetings I have sat in, in which the vast majority of people have agreed with a proposal but have utterly failed to engage with it or with the consequent action required. Meetings, unfortunately, tend to attract passengers. I would sometimes come away from a meeting with the prayer on my lips of 'God protect me from those who agree with me'! At least a bit of healthy conflict shows that people are engaged. Those who sit around nodding sagely but keeping quiet are the same people who will have a tendency to be absent when action needs to be taken. Worse still, they will be the ones, when the going gets a little rough, to utter the words, 'Well, of course I voted in favour; I wanted to support the vicar, but I always knew . . .'

Acquiescence is very slippery because it looks like agreement. It is important to flush it out in any way possible. I would use small-group discussion, individual conversations and easy opportunities for participation to attempt to counter it, but it is – by definition – a hard attitude to engage with. Again, though, the key is to name it for what it is – at least to yourself, if not publicly.

Engage

Two and a half cheers, then, to those who are actively engaged with the process of change. Only two and a half cheers? Yes: sorry to sound a discordant note with those who are apparently on side. It is important to be clear as to why exactly they are on side and engaging with change. The vast majority (one hopes) will be engaged because they are up for it and are convinced by it.

However, there will be those who are engaged because they are your supporters' club, because you are the leader and what you say must be right, or because 'Mrs Smith is against it, therefore I must be passionately for it'! Yes, I'm afraid that sometimes those who are thoroughly engaged with the process and issues of change can be among the most unhelpful thanks to dodgy motives, and it will of course be very important to be as realistic as possible about these people as well.

Having sounded this warning note, though, working with those who are engaged, who have caught the vision and see the possibilities, will be the fun and rewarding part of the exercise. This is where fruit will begin to ripen.

However, the question should then be addressed as to where the largest part of the change-leader's energy should be spent. To answer this I would like to offer another, complementary model.

The three-thirds model

Well, probably not three-thirds in reality, but certainly three groups. Developing the model of four responses to change that I offered above, I would like to refine this slightly by suggesting that in any change situation there are ultimately three groups. Again, it's fairly obvious when you think about it – there are those who are:

1 for change
2 against change
3 somewhere in the middle.

The tendency will be to spend time and energy either with Group 1 or Group 2. With Group 1 because the perception is that this is the group that is getting things done; this is where the energy lies, this is the group that agrees with me so it's comfortable to spend time and focus with them. Alternatively, there will be a tendency to spend time and energy with Group 2 because I need to persuade them to be on side, to offer concessions or to be pastoral to them.

However, all the time that Group 1 is being further enthused or Group 2 is being mollified, Group 3 is losing interest and wandering off. I would suggest that Group 3 is the vital group, the group where (perhaps counter-intuitively) time and energy needs to be spent.

Hopefully you will have recognized Group 1 as approximating to those who are 'engaged', Group 2 to those who 'resist' and Group 3 to the 'ignore' and 'acquiesce' people suggested above. If the three groups do split neatly into three-thirds then the situation isn't too bad (and if it's only a rump in Group 2 then there's probably a fair wind for change). In all likelihood, though, the largest group will be Group 3.

When change is first proposed, depending on how much background work has been done before proposals go to press, Group 3 could well be over 50 per cent of a small group and perhaps 90 per cent of a whole congregation. The art of managing change is that of ownership and addressing the very real question of 'What's in it for me?' Helping people to identify where they fit into a new situation, helping them to see that they have a part in it and helping them to be real, addresses the basic human tendency of asking, 'What's in it for me?'

Group 3 will be either uninterested or looking to see which way to jump. There are likely to be loud voices, often with significant influence, among those against change, and those 'somewhere in the middle' may well be listening to hear whose voice is prevailing. Now, sitting on the fence can be quite uncomfortable. Finding ways of helping people off the fence by engaging with them – and helping those in Group 1 to do the same – will not only help the process of change, but will be a relief to the fence-sitters. And as for those who are apparently ignoring the whole process, it will be about finding imaginative ways of engaging them. Ultimately, it returns, of course, to relationships.

As Group 3 is being won over, it is also possible that membership of Group 2 will also be eroded. However, there will always be those who, for strong and perhaps well argued reasons, will remain adamantly opposed to change. The challenge will be to leave space for them either to remain or to find a graceful way out.

Of course, if Group 2 is the largest group this poses some painful questions about the strength of the proposed change. It is important for any change-manager to constantly consider the possibility that he or she is wrong! But it may also be that the proposals have not been properly prepared, that the background work has not been fully undertaken.

A major part of the background work, I would suggest, is not just about clear proposals well argued; any change needs must be seen in the context of the prevailing culture of a church, organization or institution. As I suggested at the beginning of this chapter, we rarely start with a 'day-one' situation, but almost always with inherited culture which will be a hugely powerful factor.

The prevailing culture

In both the parishes where I was vicar it was a number of years into my incumbency before I fully appreciated what the inherited culture of each parish was. In each case there were, from my point of view, positive and negative factors at work in the culture, and it was only subsequently that I have discovered a language and vocabulary to describe these respective cultures. I have since discovered there have been a number of helpful ways explored to express these realities, among them that of Walter Wink (1984), who talks of the 'angel of a church'. Rick Warren (1995) and Bob Jackson (2002) also describe this phenomenon.

In my ministry I have seen a wide range of church cultures which form the DNA of churches, and these can be for good and ill. Unfortunately it tends to be the negative cultural features which stand out. One expression of culture which I found both amusing and worrying was at a church I visited as a prospective incumbent. The person showing me around proudly led me towards one corner of the church, where, she said, was the library which formed the basis of the church's book group. I was very impressed by this until I saw the books concerned, all by the publisher Mills and Boon! I decided (rightly or wrongly) not to take the job. However, this brief impression left me with real concern for the underlying culture of a church where this one factor seemed to predominate (though I am happy to admit that I may have missed something).

The sorts of major cultural influences that I have seen and experienced include churches where:

- one or two families run everything with a mafia-like grip;
- there is a consistent feeling that 'the diocese' is demanding too much money from us;
- there is an overwhelming feeling of depression;
- the vicar does everything and is totally controlling;
- we are really a social club;
- we welcome everyone, so long as they are 'one of us';
- children should be seen and not heard.

The list, of course, is endless, but what I am not talking about here is a problem that needs sorting: rather, I mean a culture which predominates a whole church and its history. Over and again in such situations we can scrape below the surface and discover that it has always been so (or so for many generations). Folk history will confirm it, but so will PCC minutes and parish magazines. In one church the issues of a mafia-like family dominating church life recurred through church records for many generations. It was not the same family, but it was almost as if the mantle, Elijah-like, had been handed on from one family to another.

Of course, the culture is often positive and may be:

- an openness to social projects
- a generosity in giving
- a genuinely welcoming outlook
- a sense of prayerfulness in worship.

Whatever the culture, though, it will be of key importance to name the various issues of which it is made up: to be real and honest about who we are and where we have come from. Identifying culture, for good and ill, sets a firm foundation for the development of a community. It will be painful, and I am sure that it will never be definitive, but anything which elucidates and names reality will strengthen the process of development, growth and fruitfulness.

One tool which can be useful in exploring and naming culture will be to carry out a History Audit.[5] This tool has been developed to help churches in a process of exploring and naming the historical themes of church, congregation and neighbourhood. Unlike a church history, which will look at the whole life of a church, a History Audit will consider the life of a church through examining the particular themes which appear to have significance in the life of the church and community. Themes might include one or more of the following:

- church attendance (electoral roll and average Sunday attendance figures)
- children and youth ministry (including numbers, focus, etc.)
- style of worship and changes in worship
- use of the church and buildings; architectural developments and changes in use
- length of stay and profiles of incumbents
- recurring themes in PCC minutes, parish magazines, etc.
- patterns of lay leadership
- issues and initiatives in outreach, mission and evangelism
- church music
- social, fundraising and other church events
- finance
- church and congregation planting
- socio-demographic changes in parish population and church congregation.

Exploring the appropriate themes historically is likely to be highly revealing of the ways in which the culture of a particular church has developed. By naming the culture, it will become much easier to understand the issues and to change, develop or work with the culture identified.

There are, of course, other ways of exploring culture. Another well-tested method is by wrestling seriously with Robert Warren's seven marks of a healthy church.[6] Using the criteria to undertake an honest and open audit of the prevailing culture of a particular church community will pay huge dividends. Other well-proven tools include Appreciative Inquiry,[7] Natural Church Development[8] and Faithworks.[9]

Clarifying purpose

The fourth part of the model I have identified for implementing effective change is that of clarifying purpose. I said earlier that the four parts of the model are not necessarily sequential, and various parts of the model can be in operation at the same time. While this is true, I would also maintain that significant work will have had to take place in the first three areas before work can begin in earnest in this fourth area. In order to be clear as to the ways forward, relationships will be well developed, vision and values named and culture and significant realities identified. As I hope I have shown, without knowing exactly who we are and what our strengths and weaknesses are it will be very hard effectively to clarify purpose.

Under this rather broad heading of 'Clarifying purpose' will be the production of some clear plan of action. Clarifying purpose, at its heart, though, is the 'So what are we going to do about it?' question. And in order to answer this question effectively, as much information as possible needs to be in place, so that purpose is well informed and realistic.

Mission Action Planning is now a generally accepted tool for parishes to use for clarifying purpose. Chew and Ireland (2009) have produced a very useful handbook outlining effective steps to make vision a reality. Using this (or similar) methodology will be an effective way of implementing change. In the introduction to our guidelines for Mission Action Planning for London Diocese I write:

> Mission Action Planning is a tried and tested way of putting flesh on to what we say of ourselves as a Church and Parish, exploring our strengths and the challenges that face us, and putting together a realistic plan for the way forward that God is calling us to.
>
> There is no one 'correct' way of producing a Mission Action Plan (MAP), but there are a number of important considerations for a MAP to be of use to a parish, rather than just a collection of grand ideas.[10]

The important thing, then, is that there are very clear and specific outcomes, and one of the best ways of ensuring that this is the case is to make certain that identifiable objectives are set, using the SMART acronym (Specific, Measurable, Achievable, Realistic and Time-bound). More detail can be found in Appendix 2, p. 135. The great thing about making goals SMART is that it's then possible to look back over a period of time and measure the distance travelled and explore the fruitfulness of what has been achieved.

Ministry development as culture change

Not only is it true that culture and culture change will be a major factor in developing ministry, then, but the equation works both ways. Developing ministry will inevitably be a major influence in culture change. Placing the development of ministry and the nurturing of Christians in discipleship at the heart of parish life will have a profound influence on how a community sees, understands and values itself. Individuals will begin to take ownership for the community: its values, its priorities, its culture.

Developing ministry will help individuals and groups to see their place in the Christian endeavour and find an appropriate role within the community and in facing the world. This will lead to new confidence and understanding; it will at the least refresh a culture, but has the potential for major culture change.

At the beginning of this chapter I mentioned the significant cultural change that I have seen taking place in the Diocese of London, where I have ministered as a priest for over 25 years (and lived for much longer). It is hard to give exact reasons as to why and how this change has occurred,[11] but part of the credit for turning an introspective, declining, factional diocese into a can-do, growing, openly focused one has been the consistent encouragement and positivity of both the present Bishop of London and his immediate predecessor. Both David Hope and now Richard Chartres have consistently given an up-beat message of hope and possibility to the clergy and people of the diocese.

Further, though, the culture change has been sustained and encouraged by an emphasis on clergy support and development, on giving space for entrepreneurship and local leadership to flourish, on developing lay ministry, and by lessening the burden placed on parishes by central initiatives and bureaucracy. The result has been steady growth in terms of both numbers and spiritual depth in churches across the capital. Those entrusted with leadership at a local level are equipped and released to undertake appropriate ministries in their local situations.

Leadership is inevitably a key factor in culture change and I have witnessed a similar transformation at a local secondary school, where a consistently positive approach to all aspects of teaching, learning and school life is modelled from the senior leadership downwards and becomes infectious. Again, many individual factors can point to culture change, but in the case of this school the valuing of the senior leadership team by the head, and of the staff by the leadership has led to a consistently positive and up-beat atmosphere in the school, with pupils flourishing. And the reality is that when new staff and new pupils arrive at the school, this can-do and positive culture awaits them and, of course, generally infects them.

Coda: prayer

In this chapter I have discussed and explored the practical ways in which culture change and developing ministry have mutually beneficial effects, leading to fruitfulness for Christian communities. However, I passionately believe that none of this can take place unless underpinned by prayer. Ultimately it is God's Church, not ours, and all fruitfulness comes from God; we are his co-workers.

And not only should the whole endeavour be underpinned by prayer, but involving the whole community in prayer for the venture will be an excellent way of encouraging ownership. How exactly this takes place is likely to be tradition-specific, but producing prayer cards, prayer leaflets or prayer points that can be put into everyone's hands – including (importantly) the housebound and those on the fringe of the church – will mean that people will know how to pray and what to pray for. They will be a part of the venture, under God.

4

Complementary approaches

> There are many who seek knowledge for the sake of knowledge: that is curiosity. There are others who desire to know in order that they may themselves be known: that is vanity. Others seek knowledge in order to sell it: that is dishonourable. But there are some who seek knowledge in order to edify others: that is love.　　　　　　　　　(St Bernard of Clairvaux)

The Church Pastoral Aid Society (CPAS),[1] the Christian mission agency which has a major commitment to resourcing churches in Britain, has a development package called Growing Leaders. I am constantly recommending this pack to churches for one simple and vital reason: the year-long development course does not presume to channel individuals into particular areas of Christian leadership (or jobs in the church), but rather aims to develop individuals in Christian leadership and then ask the question as to where their leadership skills might best serve the gospel. The risk in running this course, obviously, is that those who have taken part will feel called to exercise their Christian leadership in their place of work or a voluntary organization outside the Church. My answer to this perceived criticism is, hurrah! What an excellent risk to take.

The huge danger in developing individuals in ministry is that so often we have a job lined up which needs filling. This will be true of ordination training (there are lots of vicar-shaped holes in the Church of England to be filled) and of parish development initiatives (we need a churchwarden/pastoral visitor/worship leader, etc.).

When working with clergy and PCCs on helping them to develop a Mission Action Plan or equivalent, the question will often be raised: 'We want to do such and such, but who have we got in the parish who will do it?' I suggest that they turn the question on its head and ask: 'Who has God sent us and how can we best help them to develop their gifts and encourage them in their ministry, so that they can find their role in serving the gospel in this place?'

There is a tendency to shape ministry and mission around inherited and received patterns: this is the way that it's done because – well, this is the way that it's done! This may be because the parish has always done it this way, or this is the way the vicar learned to do it at college or from her or his training incumbent, or this is the way suggested in the latest book coming out of a 'successful' church. To ask the simple question, 'Who has God sent us?' can begin a radical reassessment of what God is calling us to in our own local situation.

In this and the next chapter I shall be exploring the ways in which we might best encourage people to develop in ministry to help them to fulfil God's call on their lives and best develop their God-given skills and talents. In this chapter I shall look at this from the perspective of the church or ministry situation, examining the elements which need to be taken into account in creating an environment to assist in the development of maturing Christian ministry. Chapter 5 will begin at the other end by asking who we are, as individuals, in Christian development.

Cork in the bottle?

One of the criticisms I have heard levelled against clergy throughout my ministry is that they act as a cork in a bottle, preventing the laity from carrying the ministry that rightly belongs to them. I have no doubt that there are some clergy who, for a variety of reasons (including their need to control or their own inadequacies), justify that accusation. The reality though, I believe, is much more complex.

As discussed previously, there can be many factors militating against the developing ministry in a local situation. These can include the prevailing culture, inherited norms, issues of control and unwillingness to commit. However, one of the biggest issues, I would suggest, is simply not knowing how to go about it. Rather than it being a deliberate attempt to 'keep the laity in their place', it may have more to do with not having the appropriate skills, knowledge and perception.

Perhaps one of the biggest mistakes I made when first a vicar happened through the best of intentions. I was determined not to be a cork in a bottle and I wanted to enable lay ministry in the parish. I decided, therefore, that confirmation preparation should be undertaken by lay people. (You've probably noticed the first part of the mistake already – *I decided* ... what *ought* to happen – this was not the major issue, however.) I therefore found two very willing volunteers to lead the confirmation group and handed it over to them. I knew that delegation was a good thing, so I delegated – and in the process set them up to fail.

Everyone was terribly nice about it, but I realized far too late that the whole thing was a disaster. I had totally failed to prepare the two people in leading small groups, in giving them appropriate material to use, in equipping them for the task. It seems such a blindingly obvious mistake from this distance, but at the time, and in my naivety, I thought I was being a good delegator. Much adult educational water has flowed through my ministry since then and I cringe in looking back, but this stark example is readily repeated in much smaller ways in parishes up and down the country.

I would like to say that I never did anything of the kind again, and perhaps I did learn a lesson in terms of scale. However, I am aware that, just in terms of expediency and apparently saving time, when a job needs doing someone is found to do the job and the job is given to them. Many years later I caused myself and the parish a lot of unnecessary hassle by encouraging a willing, but incompetent, volunteer to become church treasurer.

Clearly the role of discernment is vital and I believe that parish clergy should be good 'talent-spotters'. I shall return to this issue in the next chapter. However, the other huge element in this is that of equipping. As St Paul reminds us in his letter to the Ephesians:

> The gifts he gave were that some would be apostles, some prophets, some evangelists, some pastors and teachers, to equip the saints for the work of ministry, for building up the body of Christ, until all of us come to the unity of the faith and of the knowledge of the Son of God, to maturity, to the measure of the full stature of Christ. (Ephesians 4.11–13)

From delegation to development

Situational Leadership

In the late 1970s and 1980s two American management and leadership training consultants developed a concept which they entitled 'Situational Leadership'.[2] Ken Blanchard has subsequently built this concept into part of a large consulting enterprise, offering training in Situational Leadership.[3] The basic principle of Situational Leadership, however, is simple yet (I believe) profound. It works on the basis that a different style of leadership is required depending upon the maturity of the follower. An effective leader, then, will gauge the maturity of his or her follower(s) and adjust his or her style of leadership accordingly.

Blanchard and Paul Hersey propose four basic styles of leadership: Directing, Coaching, Supporting and Delegating.[4] Their proposition is that frequently followers (team members, employees, etc.) are approached at an inappropriate level for their maturity in terms of their role. When this happens, the result will be disengagement, frustration or bewilderment.

Directing

Telling people what to do has often had a bad press, but in many situations can be very necessary. A classic example of directive leadership is if a building is on fire; this is never a time for careful encouragement to get people out of a burning building, but rather a time for 'Get out. Now!' Further, though, however mature and intelligent a person is, if this is the first time that someone has heard a new piece of information or seen a new technique of operation, he or she will need to be told how to do it. So, Directing requires high directive and low supportive behaviour.

Coaching

The second stage is for the leader to be alongside the follower while he or she is undertaking a new task or piece of learning. Coaching may also include 'selling' or convincing the follower as to why the task or learning is important and encouraging someone in its importance. Coaching, then, requires high directive and high supportive behaviour.

Supporting

Once the follower is convinced of the importance of the task or learning and has a grasp of it, the next stage will be to offer support as people undertake it for themselves. This will be more 'hands-off' than coaching, but the leader will still be available for the follower to encourage and answer questions – generally to give support. Support will, therefore, require low directive but high supportive behaviour.

Delegating

The final stage is that of delegation, whereby the leader hands over the task, learning, etc., to the follower and it effectively 'belongs' to this person. So once a follower reaches Delegating status he or she will only require low directive and low supportive behaviour from the leader.

The maturity of the follower – specifically in relation to the task or learning – will be in direct proportion to the style of leadership of the leader. However, there are no absolutes in the model: no follower will ever bring a complete lack of maturity to a situation, neither will it ever be appropriate for a follower to be left completely alone in a situation.

The model is utterly transferable from training as a school teacher, lawyer or surgeon (and perhaps rather better than the adage common in hospitals that, in terms of surgical procedures, surgeons 'see one, do one, teach one'!), driving a car, operating machinery or occupying any position in commerce and industry. Or, indeed, being a member of a Christian community.

As with so much leadership and consultancy training work the model is, in many ways, organized common sense; but of no less value for this. In organizing the obvious, lives can be transformed. In my work in training and development I often refer to this model; over and again I have seen lights go on as experienced clergy see and understand the reality behind it working out in their own ministries.

So often, in my experience, in churches – as elsewhere – leaders may encourage followers to miss a stage(s), perhaps jumping too quickly to Delegating or getting stuck at a particular stage, notably Directing. In my example of confirmation preparation I jumped straight from Directing to Delegating, missing out the vital stages of Coaching and Supporting.

A theological model

The gospel gives us wonderful insight into developing into maturity by the way in which God-in-Christ approaches humanity. Jesus, in his ministry, encourages his followers into greater maturity.

So, for example, in terms of the Blanchard and Hersey model, Jesus begins by instructing his disciples, moves to coaching, then supports them in their own ministry and finally delegates 'all authority' at the Ascension – but 'leaves them not comfortless'. We might track this in the Gospels of Matthew and John:

The Sermon on the Mount (Matthew 5)

> When Jesus saw the crowds, he went up the mountain; and after he sat down, his disciples came to him. Then he began to speak, and taught them. (Matthew 5.1–2)

In the Sermon in the Mount we find a straight piece of directive teaching. The clear implication for a disciple of Jesus is that if you want to follow Jesus here is a set of teaching that it is crucial you accept. The Sermon on the Mount offers a way of seeing the world and a set of priorities which are crucial to being a follower of Jesus. Quite simply, follow this teaching and follow me; ignore this teaching and look elsewhere.

The Sending out of the Twelve (Matthew 10)

> Then Jesus summoned his twelve disciples and gave them authority over unclean spirits, to cast them out, and to cure every disease and every sickness . . . These twelve Jesus sent out with the following instructions. (Matthew 10.1, 5)

We now find Jesus moving into what Blanchard and Hersey would describe as Coaching mode. Having followed Jesus, watched and been a part of his ministry and listened to his teaching, the disciples are now being given the first taste of ministry themselves. They are entrusted and empowered with a ministry of healing and proclamation in their own right. However, Matthew spends the whole of Chapter 10 with Jesus describing the parameters of the ministry. Further, it is clear from subsequent events that the ministry they are exercising is in close proximity to Jesus' own ministry.

Blanchard and Hersey's description of Coaching mode, as high directive and high supportive behaviour, fits very comfortably with this picture painted by Matthew.

Post-resurrection appearances (John 20 and 21)

When they had finished breakfast, Jesus said to Simon Peter, 'Simon son of John, do you love me more than these?' He said to him, 'Yes, Lord; you know that I love you.' Jesus said to him, 'Feed my lambs.' (John 21.15)

We now have to turn to John's Gospel to find accounts of Jesus' post-resurrection appearances. The disciples have lived through a great deal in being with Jesus. They have learnt as much through experience as through teaching. In a period traditionally accepted by the Church as 40 days, Jesus moves into a supportive leadership role. He comes and goes, and makes it very plain that things have radically changed; he hasn't just come back to be with them as he was before. Jesus is giving the disciples the space to work things out for themselves while at the same time being there for them. Low directive, high supportive behaviour; the disciples have matured.

The Great Commission (Matthew 28.16–end)

Go therefore and make disciples of all nations, baptizing them in the name of the Father and of the Son and of the Holy Spirit, and teaching them to obey everything that I have commanded you. And remember, I am with you always, to the end of the age. (Matthew 28.19–20)

The account of the Ascension and the Great Commission is perhaps the greatest story of delegation ever told. Jesus has spent three years preparing 12 – now 11 – people to carry on his work after he leaves them. He teaches them by word and example, directing them in the good news of God's reign. Jesus coaches the disciples by encouraging them to take a share in his ministry, and gradually, with major life-changing and maturing experiences, he moves from a coaching to a supporting role. Now he delegates: he hands over 'all authority' to them but, showing his perfect leadership qualities, he ends with the words, 'I am with you always, to the end of the age.' Jesus prepares the disciples for ministry and mission and then trusts them to get on and do it; the Ascension is God's great letting-go. For Blanchard and Hersey this is clearly low (but not *no*) directiveness and low (but again, not *no*) supportiveness.

The story, then, of the Incarnation, of God coming among us in human form, is the story of perfect leadership. However, this pattern of leadership can find many parallels in the Bible, from the story of Moses through to the story of St Paul, with patterns which might be identified with Blanchard and Hersey's model.

Practical application

In applying and using the Situational Leadership model in Christian ministry, however, I find that it can be built on and developed into a very helpful sequence which will be adaptable to any given ministerial situation. I propose a six-stage model which I suggest can be drawn out in Jesus' relationship with his disciples, but also seen in action in the Church today. A process which we find on the road from first steps towards ordained ministry to being an incumbent is transferable to any form of Christian ministry. The stages are:

1 invitation and/or call
2 envisioning
3 training and education
4 coaching
5 supporting
6 delegating.

Invitation and call

As Christians we believe that we are called into ministry by God. But this calling can take place in many and varied ways.

One of the most frequent ways is by invitation. I talk elsewhere of calling, vocation and discernment, but for the benefit of this section this is simply about the practical way in which an individual begins a new venture.

The call to ministry can certainly come directly from God, but very often it is by God speaking through others. This can be anything from a chance remark to a sermon preached or a direct invitation or request. There can be little doubt that an invitation by the church leader can carry enormous weight, and particularly so if it is carefully considered and appropriate. If an invitation feels burdensome, is a way of getting a job done or is just yet another request among so many, then of course it will seem unwelcome.

However, I believe that one of the key tasks of a church leader is that of 'talent-spotter'. Although I know very little about football I would imagine that a talent-spotter who goes around minor league football clubs looking for new talent is seeking far more than fancy footwork. A good talent-spotter will be after commitment, physical fitness, team work, understanding and enthusiasm as well as skill. Without these vital ingredients there will be no capacity to stay the course.

So it is with the church leader; the reality is that asking an accountant to be church treasurer or a teacher to lead the children's work could be disastrous. He or she will have the skills to do the job, may well find it hard to say no, but there could well be an inward groan of 'I do this all week and now you want me to do it in my evenings and weekends too.' Skills without enthusiasm and commitment will be dead.

So, the talent-spotter's job is to look beyond the presenting facts and to see potential: to see the bigger picture, not just the obvious.

But of course it's not simply by invitation that people explore what God wants of them. Giving space and encouragement for individuals to explore God's calling is of huge importance. It will be through sermons which invite people to consider their calling under God; through the opening up of possibilities perhaps through pew leaflets and parish magazines; through running courses and offering exploration days – locally or at a deanery, diocesan or other wider level. An example of such a course specifically aimed at helping people to discover their Christian vocation and calling is the SHAPE course[5] designed by Amiel Osmaston, Director of Ministry in the Carlisle Diocese.

So, the first stage will not be just about finding people to fill jobs, but rather it is a three-way process of offering opportunities for individuals to discover and explore their vocation and calling; of discernment and talent-spotting; and of seeking the guidance of the Holy Spirit and creating the space for the Holy Spirit to move in people's lives and in the situation.

Envisioning

A story is told of President Kennedy visiting the Space Center at the height of the race to get a man on the moon, to 'rally the troops'. He does the classic thing of being introduced to representatives of various parts of the endeavour. Meeting each, he asks, 'And what do you do?' One says he is an astronaut, another an aeronautical engineer, yet another the mission controller, right the way down the line until he reaches the very last man. This man cleans the toilets around Mission Control. The President walks up to him and says, 'And what do you do?' The man replies, 'Mr President, I am a part of the team which will put the first man on the moon.' This man had caught the vision and saw himself as a vital part of a greater reality.

There is a huge danger when someone is invited to take on or takes on a new ministry in God's Church that it is seen in isolation rather than as a part of a greater whole.

There is, I believe, a fine balance to be sought in the process of envisioning between including someone as a part of a vision which is already in place and in encouraging and helping him or her to be a part of that vision. Ultimately it is about ownership. Clearly if the PCC has spent a great deal of time creating a

Mission Action Plan it would be highly inappropriate to go back to square one if a new person is seeking his or her ministry and place. However, it would also be unhelpful to present a ready-made vision and work out how the individual fitted in. Rather, there needs to be a degree of flexibility. In part it will be about 'selling' the vision; helping someone to see how he or she fits into a larger picture and how important his or her place is in the venture. But in order for people to 'own' the vision and their place within it, there will need to be space for their place to be shaped like them. For some people the 'shaping' process will be more important than for others.

Take the example of a new treasurer. Clearly someone coming into this role will need some experience and/or aptitude for working with figures. But being treasurer of a church is not the same as being an accountant for a large financial institution or being treasurer of the local cricket club. On the one hand, the new treasurer will need to be clear about the 'why' as much as the 'how'. Why does the church need funds? What is the big vision? On the other hand, the newcomer will need the space to adapt the role, to some extent, to suit his or her competencies and time commitments. But ultimately the church will best be served by a treasurer who owns and is a part of the vision of the church.

And this will be true, too, of anyone undertaking ministry in a church community, whether lay minister, children's worker, churchwarden, parish administrator or caretaker. Envisioning, at an early stage, is crucial to full and appropriate participation in the enterprise, into the mission and ministry of God's Church.

Training and education

It seems obvious that anyone undertaking a new role or ministry should receive appropriate training and education for the role; it seems obvious, but in my experience it is often omitted when people take on new roles in a church. Churchwardens will be given a set of keys and expected to get on with it; Sunday

School leaders will be given a bag of resources and with luck pointed to the diocesan resources; PCC members are given meeting dates and expected to pick it up as they go along.

There is no ministry in the Church of God which does not deserve appropriate training and education. And it is both training *and* education, not either/or. I learned this very early on as a rookie vicar when I asked the diocesan lay training officer to spend a Saturday morning working with those who read in church. I was expecting her to begin with voice projection lessons or how to pace the reading, but rather she sat the small group down and began a Bible study on the passage which was going to be used for that morning's training session. The message was quite simple: how can you hope to read clearly and confidently unless you understand something of what you are reading?

Again, it is starting with the 'why' rather than the 'how' of ministry. It seems so often that we understand this principle when we are training clergy – and Readers and Licensed Lay Ministers – but forget it with other ministries in the church.

There is no ministry within the church – or the wider community – which doesn't deserve background education in the 'why'. For example, I believe passionately that deanery meetings of treasurers would always do well to begin with Bible study and education in the 'why' of church finances, but it's not easy to persuade others of this. 'Why' helps people to see themselves in the larger picture; helps to give context; enables God's ministers to move from a mechanistic approach of needing to get a job done to an organic approach of seeing their ministry in the context of the mission and ministry of their church: the work of God.

As discussed above, equipping for a role, a ministry, is vitally important, but the equipping goes beyond the acquiring or sharpening of the necessary skills. Equipping means education into the context of the ministry and ministry situation, theologically and otherwise as appropriate.

Coaching

But it doesn't stop there. Coaching is now generally understood as a key element of encouraging and supporting someone in any new job and when undertaking new tasks. Indeed, major companies pay large amounts of money for the coaching of their senior executives. This process of walking alongside, in a supportive and gently challenging framework, during the initial stages of a new ministry can pay huge dividends in terms of the continuing commitment to ministry and clarity in role.

The nature of coaching will vary enormously depending upon the person and his or her experience, the role and context. Importantly, though, it will be personal and specific, and it will be scheduled. The underlying principle of coaching someone new to role or task is that that person is helped to feel secure and to know that there is a clear and defined reference point. A simple 'Let me know if you have any questions' is wholly inadequate in the initial stages, partly because we don't know what we don't know and also because for most people the tendency is to muddle through – 'I didn't like to bother you.' Coaching sessions will allow for what might seem to be simple or obvious questions, but will also give opportunity to place the ministry in the wider context of the mission of God's Church. The role of the coach in this situation will be to walk alongside the new minister.

Support

Where coaching in this context is likely to be time-limited – perhaps two or three sessions – support will be on-going. It will include clear opportunities to refer back as well as brief conversations, emails, etc., asking how it's going. The most important feature of this stage will be an appropriately open door with encouragement and opportunities for development.

It may be that the person new to ministry will have grasped the fundamental principles but will need to be encouraged to see ways of developing the role. The continuing conversation will open out the ministry and help the individual to develop ownership within the framework of the larger picture.

Delegation

Through following the process described, delegation won't be an event – as of 'Today it's all yours' – but rather a natural and organic culmination. There will probably be no actual point at which ministry is delegated, but rather it will be when the individual feels at home in the ministry and fits comfortably into the ministry team or grouping.

What delegation does not mean, however, is that the leader takes no further interest in the ministry. There will be continuing support, development and integration in terms of regular meetings, development opportunities and, where appropriate, supervision or mentoring sessions – depending upon the type of ministry.

So what would this process look like in practical terms? Let's take two very different ministries and walk through possible steps.

Practically . . . a PCC secretary, for example

John has recently retired from working in a bank. He is used to meetings and is keen to get stuck into a new ministry at church, and has offered himself as PCC secretary (to everyone's relief, as there were no other volunteers). John has been fairly fringe to the church until now, but is attending more regularly since his retirement.

The first step will be to explore with John whether this really is where his Christian calling lies or whether, rather, it's a hole he sees or thinks he can fill. This is risky for a start, particularly as the church is in dire need of a PCC secretary and he seems to fit the bill well. However, being honest and open now could save a great deal of frustration, problems or heartache later. So John needs to be clear what's involved, what the commitment might be and how long he will be expected to take it on for.

(So often when people take on a new ministry or task in a church, there is an open-endedness in the expectations. At the very least there should be an expectation of review after a period. No one should ever be expected to carry on until they drop.) The vicar (or other) needs to help John discern whether this is his calling and whether this is where the best use of his gifts, skills and enthusiasms lies.

The next step will be to help John to see the work of PCC secretary within the wider mission of the church locally and in the greater context. It will be vital that John is fully aware of the parish Mission Action Plan (or equivalent) and that he can 'find himself' in it. It will involve more than just a one-to-one meeting with the vicar and will include others to share the vision of the church. What will be important at this stage is to ensure that John doesn't think it's just about taking minutes of a meeting; there will always be those who 'do meetings', and for whom a meeting at a bank is the same as a meeting at the church is the same as a meeting at the cricket club – and therefore minutes are minutes.

In order for a PCC secretary to be really effective (or treasurer or committee chair or ordinary member) I am convinced that John will need to see the work in the context of the gospel and in the context of the vision of the local church. This will necessarily inform the way that the work and ministry is carried out.

Once John sees the work of PCC secretary in the context of the vision and mission of the church, it will be important to assess what sort of training and education he will need. Obviously he will need the skills of note-taker and summarizer, which he may or may not have from his bank work (and it should never be assumed that he has; he may have been in management for a long time and had someone else to do it for him). Imagination may be needed if additional skills are required, but diocesan staff may be helpful here (the diocesan synodical secretary or the archdeacon's PA, for example). John will also need to be able to find his way around church structures to some extent.

Importantly, though, as John has been on the fringe of church it may well be that he needs to be encouraged to undertake a process evangelism course (Alpha, Emmaus, etc.) or an Education for Discipleship course. If he is to be dealing with the things of God, the things of the Church, John will need to have some understanding of his faith and to be encouraged to develop it. A PCC secretary can potentially have an enormous influence on the shape of meetings and the priorities of the church; to have a clear understanding of the context – which ultimately is the gospel of Jesus Christ – will mean that the role will be seen as far more than just getting a job done. Efficient and appropriate administration is a spiritual matter. It will value members and include them in the process of the work of the Church.

Time spent going through minutes, correspondence and other PCC administration with John in the early stages – coaching – and helping him to see why certain emphases or nuances are important will pay huge dividends in the long run. John will become immersed in the developing culture of the church. This is the way we do things here, and this is why we do things this way.

And as John grows into the ministry he will require support, perhaps only at the end of the phone or by email, but as he feels supported so he will feel able to shape the ministry within the overall vision, bringing his gifts to it.

This sounds a lot of work to get to the point of delegation, but I am convinced that to take this process seriously would save many a parish conflict from taking place – and actually save time and energy in the long run. John knows what he's taking on, he knows why he's taking it on and what the context is, and he understands the background to the ministry. Further, he knows where to go for help and is aware that the incumbent and others take the ministry seriously. And finally, he can begin to shape the ministry, under the guidance of the Holy Spirit, bringing to bear his individual skills and talents. He will be fulfilled in the ministry and the church will benefit.

Or a lay pastoral minister

Increasingly churches are encouraging members of their congregations to assist in and contribute to the pastoral ministry of the church in a more formalized way. Dioceses are running training schemes for pastoral assistants and offering training for pastoral care teams in churches. These two different but complementary approaches show clearly that invitation and call are both appropriate starting points for individuals in taking on new ministries.

The first stage may well be that a church recognizes that it needs to respond in a broader way to pastoral care than just relying on the vicar to do it all (see Chapter 2). So it may be that a general invitation may go out for people who would be interested in taking part in a pastoral care scheme. However, experience suggests that general invitations apply to everyone else except me! (Or, even more difficult to handle, to the very people who perhaps don't have the best gifts in the field of pastoral sensitivity.) In reality it will almost always be the role of the incumbent to act as talent-spotter here, inviting those who seem most appropriate to take part.

Alternatively, it may be that an individual has a calling to take a fuller and more defined role in pastoral ministry – or that the incumbent recognizes the pastoral potential of an individual and invites that person to consider undertaking the role of a lay pastoral minister.

Clearly, in both of these scenarios there are a wide variety of combinations. But let's take Mary, whose last child has just left home and who is beginning to wonder what God is calling her to in the next stage of her life. It is relatively unlikely that Mary will book an appointment with the vicar and say, 'I think I have a vocation to be a pastoral assistant, what's the next step?' (Unlikely, though not impossible – particularly if a course has been advertised.) The more likely scenario is a chance conversation at the back of church one Sunday, or bumping into Mary in the hospital where she's visiting a neighbour, or Mary just suddenly being around more. An incumbent's antennae need to be finely tuned to notice these sorts of signals.

So it may be that Mary feels a call and comes to see the vicar, but let's assume that the vicar picks something up and suggests a conversation. It will be most likely that a Mary-shaped hole will already be beginning to take shape in the vicar's mind, but the danger is jumping too quickly to conclusions. Mary may just be too ready to accept anything that's offered, or be flattered by the approach, or assume that what is being offered may be all that is available.

So, if Mary is interested in pursuing some form of ministry within the church, a period of discernment is required. This may be very quick – go away and think about it (with a very clear open door and the clear acknowledgement that this may not be right) and agreement on both sides to pray about it. It may, though, be a much longer period of discernment, which could include attending a preliminary course (a diocesan Christian studies course, a locally run CPAS Growing Leaders course or SHAPE course, perhaps run with a number of other local churches, etc.). Patience in allowing space for the Holy Spirit to shape Mary's vocation and calling can be frustrating when there's a job to be done, but once again it will pay enormous dividends in the long run. Mary will have a clear context for her calling, it will be theologically informed and her commitment will, therefore, be much greater.

The outcome of this process, then, is that Mary is committed to the idea of being involved in the pastoral ministry of the church. The next question is: in what capacity? Might she lead a pastoral care group for the whole parish? Might she carry out one or two visits a month to the housebound, maybe assisting with communion to the sick? Perhaps it's regular care of the congregation? Or liaising with the local health and social services?

Assisting in the local hospital chaplaincy team? A specialist ministry in bereavement counselling? Being involved in the healing ministry of the church? Or a combination of these and/ or of many other possibilities?

The decision will not take place immediately, but will be a process with two very clear priorities in mind. The first, of course, will be Mary's skills, talents, gifting, personal preferences and availability. The second, though, will be local needs. If Mary feels called to visit the housebound and the church already has six people doing this, she may soon become frustrated or irritated at not being 'used' and/or will quickly be treading on other people's toes. Similarly, if the vicar is not prepared to let go of pastoral care in a meaningful way, or is not prepared to educate the parish in a new way of working, then Mary could well be being set up to fail. At this early stage the vicar has to be honest with him or herself, at the same time as encouraging Mary in her vocation and ministry.

There is also a danger that if Mary is asked to be involved in all aspects of pastoral ministry, this will exclude others and build an empire for Mary to rule with a rod of iron if she is so inclined.

So, after a careful discernment process of Mary's skills, enthusiasms and time availability and of the needs of the parish, Mary is to lead a brand new parish visiting team, to ensure that all members of the church community, at the centre and on the fringe, are pastorally cared for. That is the vision beginning to form, at least: Mary is delighted by the idea, showing a real aptitude for this, including potential leadership skills and pastoral sensitivity, and it fulfils a vital need in the parish, particularly as the vicar has just been asked to take on a diocesan role in addition to her parish duties.

Hopefully, even at this still fairly early stage the vicar will have done her homework and this idea of a parish visiting team will not only fit well within the Mission Action Plan, but will also at least be assented to by those in leadership within the parish.

So the next stage will be to put flesh on the vision; this can be done in a whole variety of ways (perhaps with and perhaps without Mary's name being associated with the vision). The process of envisioning is likely to include PCC discussion, Bible study or Lent groups, sermons, discussion in the groups that naturally meet in church (anything from formal home groups to choir or church cleaners or lunch club) and crucially individual conversations with those it will be important to have on side.

While this is taking place, it may be that Mary is being trained on a diocesan pastoral assistants' course or equivalent, or taking part in other training and preparation.

Once the vision is agreed and clear aims and objectives associated with it, the next stage will be to recruit a group of lay pastoral assistants who buy into the vision and to be clear about the expectations and commitment (and the back-door escape route). A training course will then be devised or imported which will, importantly, include a high level of discussion and agreement as to how the group is going to function as well as the development of skills and support structures.

Mary now runs the team. She meets with them once a month and encourages discussion, prayer and a degree of supervision (for which she has also had some training). Job done, and the vicar has delegated? Well, no. The vicar's role will now be to coach and then support Mary in her role (or find someone else to do this). And although Mary will require more of this at the early stages, the support and perhaps the coaching will never disappear completely.

Further, as the vision for the parish changes and grows it will be important for Mary to be a part of the envisioning process, to be clear how pastoral care fits into the larger picture, and also for Mary's perspective to be a part of the envisioning process.

Not a linear process

Although these two examples present, pretty much, as a linear process, this is clearly not the case. Each example will be taking place not in isolation but rather in front of the backdrop of normal parish life, with many other factors at play. Further, what these examples show is that the process will involve various stages taking place as and when required. Envisioning and invitation are, for example, most obviously interchangeable as the first stage. Training, education, coaching and support can be continuous and/or can be interposed at various stages of the process, and certainly after delegation has taken place. And indeed, some training and education may well take place as a part of the discernment process (as suggested in Mary's case). Further, a number of the stages may well be taking place at the same time.

Every parish is different

Just as with these two examples an approach was necessarily tailored to the individual's needs, skills and situation, so, clearly, the approaches and possibilities will need to be tailored according to the type of parish, its context, expectations, size and complexity. An inner-city parish will need different approaches and expectations from a rural multi-parish benefice or a suburban parish. Catholic parishes will have different expectations and baggage from a middle-of-the-road or a charismatic evangelical parish. Congregations with a usual Sunday attendance of 20 or 80 or 200 will all require varied approaches.

What I would maintain, though, is that the overall concept is universal; it just needs tailoring to the local situation. The examples I gave above are, of course, fairly easy ones to work with and would probably resonate well in a suburban or town parish. In both parishes where I was vicar, one inner-city, one suburban, we established a pastoral care team. The result in each case was appropriate to the context (at least, I felt it was!), but the route by which we got there was very different. At each stage, from invitation and call through to delegation, the approach was different and tailored to suit the needs and expectations of the context. Differing amounts and styles of training and education were offered to suit (one was a book and diary culture, the other neither). In one parish I was able to delegate leading the pastoral care team almost completely to a member of the laity; in the other it was important for me as vicar to be the team leader. And so on . . .

Again, it should be seen as an organic process, not one which has a template to be delivered mechanistically; the process, though, can, I firmly believe, be universally applied.

From how to what and why

So far I have looked at the importance of careful preparation in encouraging people into ministerial responsibilities, but the models I have presented suggest a strong emphasis on the teaching of skills. However, to establish and encourage a culture where people naturally wish to pursue their Christian vocation and calling, much background work will also need to take place in order for individuals to catch a larger vision of the kingdom of God and what God is asking of his disciples in this particular context.

The foundational work will move from evangelism to the making of disciples. In my experience, many parishes are good at process evangelism, undertaking courses such as Alpha and Emmaus and using many and various local mission initiatives. But the next stage of growing disciples often seems to be so much more difficult. Of course, Sunday church will be an important way of leading new Christians into discipleship, but it is, I contend, insufficient on its own.

In today's busy world, where individuals' levels of commitment tend to be low and pressures of work, family, caring and other attractions and pressures are huge, great imagination needs to be employed to find a variety of ways to develop new disciples. There are many and various short, medium and longer courses available, as well as other imaginative ideas – and I don't intend to survey or recommend any here. It is more the principle of offering a variety of context-appropriate initiatives under the general heading of Education for Discipleship that I am suggesting will be necessary to create an environment in which Christian ministry flourishes.

Course in Christian studies

One example that I am encouraging and promoting now is taken from Chelmsford Diocese and the hard work of Philip Ritchie and others. Many dioceses do, I know, have similar models and many churches run their own versions.

The Chelmsford Diocesan course in Christian studies is an excellent example of good practice, in my view, because it is both flexible and non-directive. Like Growing Leaders (discussed in Chapter 4) it is not expecting participants to take on a specific ministry or directing them into it: actually not into any ministry at all. Rather, it is about educating participants into the Christian faith. The two-year certificate-level course is accessible to participants from both a book and a non-book culture and there is the option of undertaking assignments (essays, etc.) or not. Importantly, though, it is run locally in a cluster of neighbouring parishes, using a team of three local tutors (who will usually be clergy, Readers, Licensed Lay Ministers, etc., and who will need little training themselves as the material is all provided).

Towards the end of the course there is a module on vocation, and it is at this point that participants will be beginning to ask, 'What next?' Again, there is no pressure, but the experience of more than 20 years in Chelmsford Diocese shows that large numbers of the participants go on into some form of Christian ministry.

Two years will be a huge commitment to many people, but this can be counterbalanced by the practical benefits of undertaking the course locally, with friends, but at the same time doing something which has a broader (diocesan) recognition.

But not all such courses will be so demanding. In the Stepney area of London Diocese, for example, a much shorter, very flexible course is offered to parishes. New Step runs over a shorter period (approximately two terms), has optional modules which can be chosen by the participants, and offers a combination of practical discipleship and Christian education in a non-book culture.

Ultimately, however, the benefit of this (and other similar variations on the same theme) is that they are organic in process, allowing participants to find themselves in the Christian story and to understand Christian mission and ministry from the wider perspective of the story of their faith. The commitment of participants will be informed and encouraged by being immersed, with other fellow-travellers, in a rounded education for their discipleship in Jesus Christ.

Conclusion

The approach that I recommend in this chapter, then, can seem very frustrating and long-winded. I know only too well the reality of a churchwarden resigning and the sinking feeling of there being no obvious candidate to succeed. I also know the hard work and frustration when grabbing a willing 'victim' to fill a hole only to find that he or she is far from appropriate to role and task.

Working organically does not produce quick results, but it does build deep and secure foundations. Jesus told a relevant parable about houses built on sand and on rock.

5

What am I like?

The gifts he gave were that some would be apostles, some prophets, some evangelists, some pastors and teachers, to equip the saints for the work of ministry, for building up the body of Christ.   (Ephesians 4.11–12)

Have you noticed that computers, mobile phones, cameras, and so on, no longer have instruction manuals with them? No, I hadn't either! I have just told you a hugely important piece of information about myself. There will be many people reading this who will be enormously frustrated by the fact that instruction manuals don't come with gadgets any more (like my wife) and those, like me, who will have hardly noticed.

Typically, when a new piece of equipment arrives in our house I will open the box and immediately try to see how it works. My wife will dive for the instruction manual, if there is one, or go on to the web to find something. My preferred learning style is that of an Activist – I simply want to get on with it, and so am just as likely to break it or miss some vital link in setting up. My wife's preferred learning style is Theorist – she wants to know all about it and can spend hours curled up with a handbook (and is she ever going to use it?).

I am, of course, caricaturing, and usually my wife and I see our differing learning preferences as wonderfully complementary (though there have been moments . . .). Learning preferences are, of course, just that – preferences. They are not boxes in which we sit, unable to work or live in other ways. As developing human beings we will be able to live and work in a whole variety of different ways, but we will all have tendencies to do or understand things in different ways.

In this chapter I am going to explore briefly – and certainly not in any detail – a number of areas of preference that we may have as individuals. I shall do this simply to help consider the reality that we are all different and should be treated differently.

There are any number of 'categorization' tools readily available, such as Myers-Briggs, Belbin, Enneagram, DiSC, Strengthsfinder and many others. What I don't propose to do in this book is discuss their individual merits or uses, but I do believe that the vast majority have their benefits, though none can tell us how to live our lives. If you want to find out about these or others a quick internet search will give you more information than you can possibly want.

What I shall do, though, is look at four areas of the human situation which are often summed up as strengths and weaknesses (or more positively as strengths and opportunities). Each of the four areas has had many books written about it and there are professionals who work in each field to develop and assist individuals in benefiting from understanding themselves better. For the purposes of this book, however, my sole intention is to help in raising awareness that we are all different in our approaches and it is necessary to take this into account when working in Christian development.

By way of illustration, I get very frustrated by the number of books written in the field of prayer and spirituality which effectively say, 'This is the way to pray.' 'No, it isn't,' I want to scream back at the author, 'it is one way that *you* have found helpful to pray.' I am attracted to books on spirituality which say (or clearly imply), 'I have discovered this way of praying which I have found particularly helpful at this point on my journey; I offer it to you [the reader] as you too may find it helpful.'

The world is full of self-help books, how-to-do-it books and get-rich-quick books, some of which completely fail (deliberately or through stupidity) to understand or acknowledge that we are all different and that what works for one will not necessarily work for others. It may have worked for you, but why would it work for me?

Learning styles and preferences

One of the most important factors, then, in providing any form of Christian education, training and development is to recognize that participants will, possibly without realizing it, approach what is being offered in terms of their preferred learning style. Being an activist by nature I will jump straight in and say what I mean by this (but don't worry, reflectors, theorists and pragmatists, I'll satisfy your learning preferences in due course).

So, there are basically four learning styles, activist, pragmatist, reflector and theorist. We all use all of them to some extent, but the clear suggestion is that everyone has a preference for one of these styles, usually with a second preference not far behind. Someone with an activist preference (as I've already suggested) will tend to want to get on with a new piece of learning and see what it does. A pragmatist will want to know why – why are we learning this? What are the practical implications of this piece of learning? A theorist will need to know the background, the evidence, the sources for this piece of learning. And a reflector will need time to assimilate and reflect on the learning in order to contextualize and place it appropriately.

A simple example of this might be buying a bicycle. The activist would tend to go into the nearest cycle shop, buy a bike which looks about right, jump on it and away he or she goes. The pragmatist would consider what exactly he or she was going to use the bike for and buy one for its suitability for those needs. The reflector might take time in considering the nature of cycling, how it fitted into his or her lifestyle and what cycling said about him or her as a person. The theorist might take a long time researching various bicycles, comparing prices, relative strengths and weaknesses of different models and exploring the best ways of riding one for a range of benefits.

A cynic might suggest, however, that the activist would buy a dud, the pragmatist wouldn't have any fun, the reflector's bike would sit in the shed waiting for the ideal cycling conditions and the theorist wouldn't get around to buying one, having so much fun doing the research!

Now the theorists will be asking: where does all this come from? What is your basis for writing this? Well, the two key texts are by Kolb (1984) and Honey and Mumford (1986). David Kolb first articulated the learning cycle and his seminal work is now the basis for much adult learning. He demonstrates that for learning to take place it needs to be approached and offered from a cycle which includes all four ways of assimilating and absorbing new information. Peter Honey and Alan Mumford developed this cycle to show that each of us has a preferred learning style. This work has been well presented in Lamdin and Tilley (2007, pp. 56–63). It can also be found in summary form on a free website, Businessballs.[1]

The 'so what' in this (for the pragmatists) is that we have a tendency to present new learning, training and development in a way which suits ourselves. It will be crucial in any education, training and development that we have all bases covered or we're likely to lose people at an early stage. As an inveterate activist I have a tendency to lose theorists, because I'm in danger of forgetting the importance for them of producing the evidence to support my teaching.

As a vicar, this truth became very apparent to me when leading PCC meetings. When a new idea was introduced the activists either wanted to get on with it or reject it out of hand, the pragmatists wanted to know why and to see the connections, the reflectors needed to go away and think about it and the theorists wanted evidence, research and precedent.

What we don't need to know, necessarily, is who fits into each neat box – because the boxes won't be neat – but rather we must just ensure that we have something on offer for each learning style, as this will not only address learning preferences but will also give a rounded approach to learning.

Personality preferences

A good few years ago a religious community I knew well decided to undertake a Myers-Briggs Personality Type Indicator® workshop. The whole community duly took part and everyone was given their personality type. A couple of weeks later one of the community told me how appalled she had been by the whole experience and what a terrible thing Myers-Briggs was. I was shocked, being a bit of a fan of it myself. As the conversation developed, however, the issue was not with Myers-Briggs itself, but rather with how it was being used. Members of the community were 'boxing' one another up. So-and-so had only done this or that because she's an ... (insert personality type). In a sense members of the community were ceasing to see one another as individuals made in the image and likeness of God, but rather as personality types, predestined to do things in certain ways.

Being a very healthy religious community, they speedily identified the problem and rectified it through discussion, deliberation and prayer. However, the issue helped me to understand how easily such tools can be misused. The fundamental point is that all profiling tools are descriptive and not prescriptive. In other words, they are only tools which help to describe preferences and tendencies: they are not about putting people into boxes, prescribing how they will act and react in any given situation.

Although I remain a fan of Myers-Briggs some 25 years after I first attended a workshop, I do take issue with the vocabulary which is often used of the process. I am much more comfortable with the term 'personality preference', so that it then describes my preferred response in a situation, rather than implying a pre-ordained response.

If you are unfamiliar with tools such as Myers-Briggs, the Enneagram and others – I am not going to go into great detail about them here – research them on the web to find out more; there is a wealth of information available. Once again, I discuss them simply to underline the importance of taking differing personalities seriously.

A really obvious example of this is the fact that everyone is on an introvert–extrovert scale. There is nothing wrong with being one or the other, and I do believe that we can change and move on the scale depending upon circumstance and what is going on in our lives. However, when organizing education, training and development there will be those who relish working in small groups, who will have no problems asking questions in larger groups and who will chat happily in coffee breaks; these people will tend to be towards the extrovert end of the scale. Similarly there will be others who will be taking information in, tend not to speak much in large groups and may need to be drawn out in small groups, will need to have time alone to assimilate information and will want to wander off alone during coffee breaks: generally those towards the introvert side of the scale.

It's not that there's a right and a wrong way of taking part in group training and discussion; rather, people do it in different ways. Introverts may well want to get home quickly after the end of a session whereas extroverts may want to stay and chat. A very simple rule of thumb is that people whose personality preference is introvert draw energy and recharge their batteries by being alone, whereas those with an extrovert preference recharge by being with other people. However, this is simply descriptive and there will be variations and inconsistencies within this description.

Another example is that some people are 'portrait' people and some are 'landscape' people. Given a plain sheet of A4 paper with a view to taking notes or working through a problem, some people will tend to go for writing a list or text down the length of the piece of paper (portrait-fashion) and others will want to do a mind-map or draw interlinking concepts across the width of the paper (landscape-wise). Both can be perfectly valid and are just different personality preferences (and generally most people can work either way – they do just have a preference).

Once again, it is impossible to cater for each and every personality preference, and even if it were possible people don't always want to work from their preference (Jung speaks of developing one's 'shadow' or less preferenced tendencies). However, being aware and taking into account the simple notion that personalities differ will be vital in offering education, training and development.

For those who are involved in training and education I do think it is well worth undertaking one or more of these tools simply to understand how they work, to take the general principles into account and to be clear about your own preferences.[2]

Skills, gifts and passions

I love doing DIY, but I'm not very good at it; I am passionate about rugby but my games teacher at school would be very surprised to hear this; I find doing research tedious and boring but seem to come up with pretty creditable results when I undertake it. What's this all about? Quite simply, our skills, our gifts and our passions do not always coincide.

Just because I enjoy doing something doesn't mean that I'm going to be good at it (how many aspiring actors have been told, 'Don't call us . . .'?). But conversely, just because I'm good at something doesn't necessarily mean I'm going to enjoy it or feel passionate about it. It sounds obvious, but I do think we can often confuse the two.

As Christians we believe that every person has God-given gifts and talents. However, we are well aware that many people never have a chance to express those talents or do so only in a very modest way. I have sometimes at funerals heard people express the sentiment that he or she died with 'their music still in them'.

In Christian development we are aiming to deal with whole people, not just the bits of them that we find useful to the church. Why is it that when we find a teacher in church we immediately want him to help with the Sunday School? Or an accountant starts coming so we persuade her to join the finance team? Just perhaps they've had enough of teaching or accounting in their working lives; just perhaps they want to express other skills, gifts and passions. It may tick a box for the church, but is it developing them as Christians?

In employment terms Pedrick and Blanch (2011: 10ff.) talk of three elements combined in a Venn diagram:

- What skills do you have to offer? (strengths)
- What do you enjoy doing? (passions)
- What will the company/organization pay for? (needs)

Where the three coincide, it is likely that you will be happy and fulfilled in your work. But it is surprisingly rare that all these fit neatly together. A great number of people spend a great deal of their working day doing things that they may be good at – have skills to offer – and that the organization is prepared to pay them for, but it's not where their passion lies. They do it to pay the rent or mortgage.

A friend of mine is an expert and sought-after computer programmer. He is committed to his work and is well paid as a result. But he doesn't really enjoy it. What he really enjoys is music. He might have made it in the very crowded world of professional musicians, but it's certainly too late now. So he bought himself an organ on which he plays Bach and Vierne to a very high standard (to my ears, at least) and he sings in a highly professional choir. He could conduct a choir and he could be organist of a prestigious church, but this is the compromise that he's made. Not entirely satisfactory, but it works for him and his life-choices. The 'company' wouldn't pay him for making music so he expressed his passions elsewhere.

So often, I believe, people come to church looking for ways to express not just their skills but also their passions. And if they don't, we should be encouraging them to. As I discussed before, it's not just about filling the jobs we may have at church, but it is about helping the people whom God has sent us to fulfil their potential in the service of the gospel. This may include doing stuff in church, but it may equally include equipping people for ministry in other parts of their lives.

Working with clergy I am acutely aware that many have forgotten, or lost track of, their first love; what was it that originally attracted them to be a priest or pastor in the Church of God? It is really helpful, I believe, to assist clergy in revisiting their passions. The great thing about parish ministry is that clergy can and should always create space to follow their passions in ministry.

One of the ways we are addressing this in London and Chelmsford Dioceses is by running a residential course entitled 'Renewing Vision, Renewing Ministry'. The course is specifically aimed at clergy around the age of 50 years, who have been in parish ministry for a significant amount of time. The aim of the course is 'To assist clergy approaching their final phase of stipendiary ministry to assess their skills, experience and strengths, in order to set renewed vision for their ministry'. In other words, we look at how to enthuse and encourage clergy not to wind down towards retirement, but to really go for their passions in ministry, particularly now that they have a wealth of experience to support them: to step out of the mundane and rekindle the fire that was burning when they first went forward for ordination.

Such a process could well be considered in parish ministry. So often, people end up doing jobs for ever because nobody gives them permission to stop. And it may well be that they only started doing the job in the first place because there was nobody else to do it, or they were bounced into it by the vicar.

To ask the question about passion is dangerous, because people's passions may not be what they're good at or where their skills lie, but it can begin a vital conversation about how they can best fulfil their Christian vocation using their God-given gifts, talents, skills and passions – which leads us on neatly to the next section.

Vocation and call

I believe that the word 'vocation' has been hijacked in the Church to refer exclusively to ordained ministry. Many dioceses have Vocations Officers, whose job is primarily to encourage people to consider ordained ministry. This is a complete nonsense. At the heart of the Christian gospel is the concept of call; every person is called to a vocation and ministry, and each of us continues to be called throughout our lives.

The Bible is packed with examples of call, from the patriarchs through the prophets and to the disciples. Over and again we see in the Scriptures God calling individuals to fulfil their vocation and ministry. But this never begins with 'doing a job'.

God calls humanity first and foremost into being. As human beings we are made in the image and likeness of God and God calls us for himself to be the people, the individuals, that he has created us: the best possible Mary, John, Martha or Peter that we can be.

And God calls by name. God knows us individually: who we are; what we are capable of; what our strengths and our weaknesses are; our hopes and our fears. God knows me better than I know myself and he calls me.

God calls us into relationship; into relationship with God the Holy Trinity and into relationship with others; with family, with friends, with neighbours. God calls us into community with others.

God calls us to fruitfulness and to be messengers of his gospel. God calls us to mission and to bear witness; to discipleship and to engagement; to prayer and to activity; to reflection and to action.

It is through hearing and following God's call and through discovering the person that I am, within the love of God, and the place in which I am to be, that I learn and uncover what it is that I am called to do. The specific task or functions that I am called to come out of the prior callings to life and being, to relationship and community, to being known and loved for myself. And the uncovering of this is not a once-for-all event, but rather a lifetime's process and journey which will move and grow as I mature, develop in experience, wisdom and knowledge, and find myself in new situations.

It is in this context that I discover my vocation and it is in this context that we assist others in discovering their vocation. And, of course, vocation is multilayered. I may have a vocation as a teacher, but I can express that vocation in many different ways and in numerous situations. I may get paid a great deal of money for teaching as a professor in a top American university or I may teach toddlers in my spare time in the church Sunday School.

In developing Christians – and in continuing to develop ourselves – we needs must pay great attention to each person's vocation. Vocation is precious and is unique to each person. It is much more than doing a job and brings together all the other elements and attributes I have discussed in this section. Each person's vocation develops throughout his or her life; it is on-going and not once and for all. It can certainly change (and sometimes quite dramatically) because we as people change and develop and our situations, circumstances and contexts change. And, importantly, it will be multi-faceted, revealing itself in a variety of ways.

However, to keep our call and vocation alive requires discipline and responsibility. As those who are involved in enabling others to develop, we have a responsibility to assist them and to help them to be aware of the responsibility before God of nurturing and developing vocation. Vocation can be dulled or obscured by the pressures of day-to-day work and ministry. I have certainly met clergy and Christians in a whole variety of ministries whose vocation has become lost in the business of doing the job. It is important to find space in busy lives to reflect on our calling and not just on the various activities that make up our work or ministry. It will be important, too, to have someone with whom this reflection can take place.

Vocation can take us to places we would rather not go, and perhaps Jeremiah is a good example of the reluctant prophet who repeatedly goes to the places where he knows he will be hurt, abused and vilified in order to fulfil his vocation and calling.

Ultimately, though, finding, nurturing and following our vocation, and allowing it to change and develop, will be life-enhancing; will bear fruit; will lead into fullness of life.

Conclusion

As can be seen from this chapter, the 'Who am I in this venture?' question is a vital part of any development in ministry. As discussed in the previous chapter, the great danger is that we have jobs to fill and we look around for someone to fill them. As those who are encouraging others in developing in ministry, we are in the business of Christian discipleship. Jesus called as his disciples individuals with their own strengths, weaknesses and opportunities, as we can clearly see in the Gospel narratives (Peter the Rock, Matthew the Tax Collector, Simon the Zealot, Mary and Martha, James and John the Sons of Thunder, and Judas who was to betray him . . .).

Rather than beginning with 'What jobs have I got to fill?' perhaps a more exciting place to start is 'Whom has God sent and how can I help each to develop their own God-given vocation?' It may leave a few vacancies on the PCC, and it may well be a longer and more tortuous process, but my hunch is that it will bear fruit, and bear it abundantly.

6

Reflection and review

We trained hard ... but it seemed that every time we were beginning to develop as a team we would be reorganized. I was to learn later in life that we tend to meet any new situation by reorganizing; and a wonderful method it can be for creating the illusion of progress while producing confusion, inefficiency, and demoralization.

(Attributed to Gaius Petronius, *c.* AD 27–66)

I proudly tell people that I joined the Health Service in 1975, just after the 1974 reorganization, and left in 1981, just before the 1982 reorganization; a brief window of relative stability. However, I remember very clearly the above quote attached to my boss's wall above his desk. The NHS has probably suffered from more reorganization in its brief existence than any other institution in history. It often seems that the word 'review' has become a synonym for ideological change in modern parlance; in order to prove you're doing something in a political environment, reorganization is vital.

I am wholly convinced that review is necessary, but am just as convinced that it is not a euphemism for radical or inevitable change. Good leadership of an institution or situation does not necessarily mean reorganizing it.

Individual review

Without regular and systematic review bad practice can easily become institutionalized and accepted as the norm. In the overwhelming majority of churches that I work with, there will be at least one person who has been allowed to stay undertaking some prime task for too long, without check or review. I give two examples, which will be familiar to many readers.

In one church I worked with recently, the newly arrived vicar realized that one of the major issues facing the church was the quality of music on a Sunday morning. Hymns were sung painfully slowly, with poor accompaniment, because the organist was simply no longer up to the job. He was much loved and had been a faithful member of the church community for longer than anyone could remember, but he was now in his nineties. After much thought and various attempts to approach the issue from the side, the vicar realized that he must face the issue head on and inform the organist that it was time for him to retire (in the knowledge that there was no obvious replacement for him). To soften the blow he organized a party and recognition at a diocesan level for his exceptional service. However, when he finally sat down and talked with him, he discovered that the organist was delighted by the prospect of retirement and had only continued through a sense of duty. He is now fulfilling his dream of visiting other churches on a Sunday morning to enjoy their music! The issue was simply that nobody had had the courage to undertake an urgently needed and much overdue review.

However, few stories have such a happy ending. At another church the issue for the new vicar was a woman in her seventies whose whole life now revolved around running the Sunday School. The problem was that she was not only excluding all other potential leaders and helpers, but also alienating the children who attended. Further, her model of Sunday School was wholly outdated for the current situation in terms of the children's expectations and the church's mission. The vicar attempted to have a number of conversations with her, all of which were met with a brick wall. His only option was enforced and public retirement, which caused dismay within the church community and a complete lack of understanding by the person concerned; she remains a very grumpy fringe member of the church. However, her removal has liberated the children's work in the church, which is now a key point of mission in the community, attracting many unchurched children and their families.

In both cases the issues were various and complex. However, at their heart both revolve around one very simple issue: the lack of structure in appointments. And this applies to both paid and voluntary positions (in the case of these two situations, the organist's was a paid post, albeit very minimal, and the Sunday School teacher's voluntary). For generations people have been appointed to posts and ministries within churches and the unspoken expectation has been that they will continue in post for an undetermined length of time, without review and with no clear boundaries.

Many churches now give anyone who holds a ministry portfolio a job description, and certainly curates, Readers, Licensed Lay Ministers and others in formal positions will have role descriptions, work agreements or equivalent. The Royal School of Church Music (RSCM) produces a specimen contract and job description for church musicians. Under the new Clergy Terms and Conditions of Service, all clergy newly appointed to post will have a Statement of Particulars which, in practical terms, amounts to the same thing. Some might see this as the bureaucratization of the Church – and there is clearly a danger of trying to tie details of complex roles down on pieces of paper. However, there is huge benefit with the clarity that such agreements bring.

Quite simply, the above two scenarios would not have happened if clear boundaries had been established at the start of the ministries and the boundaries had been taken seriously. Clearly both had been appointed long before such ideas had been introduced, but learning lessons from history, including relatively recent history, pays huge dividends.

And what does taking boundaries seriously mean? Well, in all cases it will mean instituting and enacting a system of regular and organized review. Rather than seeing this as creeping bureaucracy, it should be seen as basic common sense.

Where regular and organized review is an expected part of the deal it will not come as a surprise when it takes place, and there will be a clear focus for discussion of issues, opportunities, problems and difficulties relating to role, on both sides. If handled well it will almost always be an affirming process as the person being reviewed will feel that he or she is being taken seriously. And if it becomes a part of the culture of a church, nobody will feel singled out; it's just 'the way we do things', part of our culture. Further, in very many cases people will take it as a normal part of life as they will be (or will have been) reviewed regularly in their workplace. For those for whom it was a negative experience at work, this can be an excellent opportunity to show what a positive experience review can be.

Review will, then:

- formalize the 'How's it going?' question;
- be a two-way conversation;
- offer possibilities for support and development;
- give opportunity for change, refocusing or expansion of role;
- ensure that no one is undertaking a ministry that he or she is unable or unwilling to continue.

The key to effective review will be in presentation. If it's seen as a 'checking up' process then it will be treated with suspicion, but if it is shown to be a positive experience of affirmation and accountability, the simple question becomes, 'Why wouldn't you want to be reviewed?'

At the head of the clergy ministerial development review (MDR) process in London Diocese are the following aim and objectives:

> The aim of ministerial reviews is that ministers should become more effective Christians in the service of Jesus Christ through self-reflection and the affirmation of their peers.
>
> The objectives are that ministers:

1 be given an opportunity to pray and reflect on their vocation and ministry;
2 take stock of their ministry thus far and identify areas on which to build and areas of need which should be given attention;
3 be given an opportunity to be encouraged and challenged;
4 become realistic about their strengths and weaknesses;
5 set goals for their work and personal development;
6 identify and access both personal and professional training, support and development needs.[1]

There is, though, nothing new about the concept of review. There is very good precedent in the Bible, and particularly in Jesus' ministry. In the London Diocesan Report on clergy MDR, mentioned above, we identified three clear theological themes pointing towards the place of review: vision, reflection and equipping.

The King James Version of the Bible has the writer of Proverbs saying, 'Where there is no vision, the people perish' (Proverbs 29.18). Although this is rendered differently in other translations, it is this translation which seems to have most familiarity and resonance. The concept of holding the big picture, of seeing further and of having a vision for what can be, under God, is shot through the Scriptures and through Christian tradition. The stories of the patriarchs are alive with vision for what might be. The prophets paint vivid pictures of the vision of God's possibilities alongside the present realities. Jesus talks constantly of a vision of the kingdom of God in his teaching and in his parables. St Paul's whole ministry is built on a vision of the good news of Jesus Christ being spread throughout the world.

Each person called to ministry in God's Church and in God's world does so as part of a greater vision. The danger can be that individuals see their particular ministry in isolation and without reference to the bigger picture. Review will offer a clear opportunity to place ministry in the context of the bigger vision:

the vision for ministry and mission of the particular church and also for the whole of God's Church. Further, though, it will also give opportunity to explore a wider vision for the area of ministry concerned; it is not just about doing a job. Rather, for example, as leader of children's ministry, how do I, how does our church, how does the Christian faith, see mission and ministry among children? What is our vision under God and how do I fit into this vision? Or, as church organist, is it just my job to turn up and play a few hymns on Sunday morning, or rather is this part of a vision for the worship and liturgy of our church to reflect God's glory and offer an environment of prayer, praise and mission to all who come?

A review, then, offers a key opportunity to see each minister's practice and area of concern in terms of the greater whole. It will encourage people to see themselves as part of a greater enterprise – nothing less, ultimately, than the vision of the kingdom of God. It will also help reviewer and reviewee to set appropriate priorities, both for the individual and for the area of ministry.

'After [Jesus] had dismissed the crowds, he went up the mountain by himself to pray' (Matthew 14.23). At significant moments in his ministry Jesus took time out to pray: notably before he began his public ministry, before he called his first disciples, at the Transfiguration before he turned his face towards Jerusalem, and in the Garden of Gethsemane before his trial and death.

Importantly, too, Jesus provided opportunities for his disciples to reflect with him. Sometimes it was briefly, explaining a parable or helping them to understand why they were unable to effect a healing. But also, more significantly, when they returned from their mission visiting nearby towns to preach the good news and after his Resurrection, before sending them out at the Ascension.

Review, then, will provide an ideal opportunity to reflect on ministry: to take time aside and to ask the crucial question of 'How's it going?' in an organized way.

> The gifts he gave were that some would be apostles, some prophets, some evangelists, some pastors and teachers, to equip the saints for the work of ministry, for building up the body of Christ, until all of us come to the unity of the faith and of the knowledge of the Son of God, to maturity, to the measure of the full stature of Christ. (Ephesians 4.11–13)

In addition to reflection and vision-building, review also gives the opportunity to explore how well God's ministers are equipped to carry out the ministry to which they are called. First, it will present the opportunity to explore whether an individual's skills, gifts and talents are a good fit with the ministry he or she is undertaking.

The reality is that situations change and individuals change depending on their life circumstances. Both of the examples given above illustrate this; we of course don't know, but it is more than possible that both the organist and the Sunday School leader were excellent at their duties when first appointed. But in both situations the circumstances changed (what was appropriate in one generation became inappropriate in another) and their own situation changed; their ageing and their perspective changed the way they carried out their duties. It should be noted here that even staying the same is a form of change when circumstances change around you.

So the pattern and the expectation of regular review should enable issues to be addressed long before they reach crisis point. A conversation can begin which may lead on to issues of the need for change; of a fresh approach; of an expansion of role; of approaching retirement. And then, rather than a feeling of being dumped and put on the scrap heap, a process of being equipped for a new ministry or new phase or season might be negotiated.

Second, though, equipping is not a one-off event, but rather a continuous process. Review will give the opportunity for a discussion about what training and development can be offered to equip someone further in ministry. It may be to enhance his or her current ministry or to expand or redirect that ministry in new directions. Investing time and money in developing and enhancing skills is likely to be highly beneficial to the whole church community, as well as helping the individual grow.

A review, then, will usually be both affirming and challenging and will be part of an on-going process which aims to build a relationship of trust and expectation between reviewee and reviewer, under God. A good review will have clear and agreed outcomes which are likely to include SMART goals.[2] These will be written down and will form part of the following review.

The 'who' of review

It is clearly the responsibility of the leader of any organization or community to ensure that appropriate review is carried out, so in a church situation the incumbent bears this responsibility. However, the incumbent doesn't necessarily need to undertake all ministry reviews him- or herself. In a small community it may well be appropriate, but in a larger community it will be necessary to find others with whom to share this responsibility. The important thing is that people are properly trained and equipped to carry out reviews sensitively.

Every diocese in the Church of England will now have a Director of Ministry, or equivalent, who will be responsible for clergy ministerial development review, for example. The advice of such people can be sought to offer training at a local level. Further, many parishes which have members who are involved in human resources or consultancy may well be prepared to 'lend' an appropriate person to assist in a parish where there are no such skills available – it can be a very simple way, with limited commitment, to share ministry between parishes of vastly differing demography (and offer learning in both directions!).

The most important factor for reviewers, however, is that they are good at listening, discerning, summarizing and reflecting.

It is certainly not a process for telling people how to do their job or undertake their ministry, neither is it an opportunity for problem-solving. Active listening is the key to good review. Ultimately, the task of a good reviewer is likely to be helping reviewees to discover for themselves where God is calling them to change, adjust or develop in their ministry, rather than telling them. The chart in Figure 3 illustrates a spectrum, and ideally I believe that the closer the review process can be to the right-hand end, the more likely the reviewee will be to own the process and for it to effect real change and development: to bear fruit.

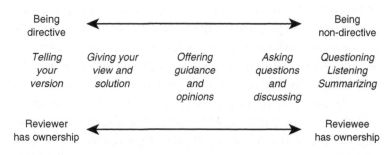

Figure 3

The 'how' of review

Review does not need to be a highly bureaucratized system of form-filling. At its simplest level it might be a conversation around a few questions, such as:

- How's it going?
- What excites you in your ministry?
- What drains you in your ministry?
- How do you think others see you in this ministry?
- How long do you see yourself undertaking this ministry?
- Where might God be calling you in the future?
- How could you be better equipped?

Importantly, these will be 'open' questions: that is, questions which develop a conversation rather than ones which beg a simple yes or no answer. (Examples of 'closed' might include, 'Is everything all right in your ministry?' Or, 'Are you enjoying what you're doing?' Such questions are in danger of closing a conversation down rather than opening it up.)

Ideally, though, a review will revolve around and/or include discussion of a job description, work agreement or role definition. Further, preparation work undertaken by the reviewee will be highly beneficial to the process, and this is likely to be in the form of some preparatory paperwork, which is submitted to the reviewer in advance of the session. The great advantage of this is that both reviewee and reviewer are given a framework within which to prepare for the review meeting. Very often the preparation work undertaken by the reviewee can be as useful as the review session itself. I know of clergy, for example, who will take a day (or more) away in a retreat environment to consider and pray about the review questions. Often, too, clergy will share the preparation with trusted friends, colleagues and/ or PCC members. All are examples of good practice, as time spent in prayerful reflection and input from others will all feed the process, enhancing the outcomes.

However, the local culture needs to be taken very seriously, and in a non-paper culture simply asking the reviewee to think about a series of questions in advance (and perhaps make some notes) may not only be more realistic, but may also make the whole process more accessible (and less intimidating for someone who is new to review). In other words, the review process should ultimately be life-enhancing, not burdensome.

When review takes place regularly as a part of a cultural expectation, there should be no great surprises in the review process. Further, so far I have described a situation which sees review as positive and beneficial. Certainly, if it is being introduced from fresh it can easily be sold as such. Inevitably, though, there will be those who will see review as a threat.

Perhaps the most important lesson in introducing review for the first time is to start with those who are 'up for it'. Pilot a review process with ministers and colleagues who can already see the benefits of it and encourage them to 'talk up' the process. If you start with the equivalents of our Sunday School leader above, it is doomed to failure. It will immediately be seen as a way of exposing someone's weaknesses or of levering someone out of a job. Once review becomes established as a positive experience and people are talking of how positive the experience is, with perhaps a presentation to the PCC and/or leadership team, then will be the time to expand the practice to all in (leading) ministry roles (it will, of course, be up to the local situation to determine exactly what roles and which people will most benefit from review). In other words, review is not a quick-fix for problematic people. Rather, its introduction can begin a cultural change to ensure that the wrong people don't get stuck in inappropriate positions in the future.

However, the review process will also provide an objective framework for the more difficult conversations. It certainly won't sort out extreme cases (these will need to be faced head on, and taking advice from those skilled in conflict resolution will be invaluable in such situations). But the great thing about established review processes is that if taken seriously by all concerned they should avoid getting into situations such as those outlined. Potentially difficult conversations which revolve around whether someone is still undertaking an appropriate ministry or may be approaching the time to hand over to someone else – or just needs a sabbatical – can be explored in a more objective and less personalized way and will be part of an on-going conversation, not suddenly appearing, as it were, out of the blue.

The 'when' of review

The most important factor in 'when' is that it should be a regular event. In other words, it should take neither the reviewee nor the reviewer by surprise, but be timetabled in. A formal review may only need to take place every second year and probably no more than annually. However, informal follow-ups may take place more often, perhaps every six months – a simple 'How's it going?' referring back to the objectives and agreed outcomes set.

The 'when', though, should also be at a mutually convenient time and in a relaxed environment. It certainly shouldn't be in a rush or crammed in before or after another meeting. Ideally an hour and a half or two hours should be allowed for the review meeting so that it can be unhurried and with an opportunity for healthy dialogue as well as agreeing outcomes.

Reflective practice

So far I have described review structures which are set up to provide the opportunity for the church or organization to review its ministers. However, good practice will also involve encouraging each minister (including ourselves) to continually review our own practice.

In his excellent work *The Reflective Practitioner* Donald Schön (1991) describes the way in which we can continually review our practices by giving space and time to reflect on the work and ministry we are undertaking.

Although Schön's work is directed at those in the professions (and he offers an interesting discussion on what constituted a profession in the early 1980s, territory which no doubt would be further debated today), the principles that he outlines are, I would suggest, wholly transferable to the field of Christian ministry.

In reflective practice, he argues, those practising professions (or Christian ministry, I would argue) can, in reflective conversation, impart and share more than can be easily described in words. In his preface he says:

I have collected a sample vignette of practice, concentrating on episodes in which a senior practitioner tries to help a junior one to learn to do something. In my analysis of these cases, I begin with the assumption that competent practitioners usually know more than they can say. They exhibit a kind of knowing-in-practice, most of which is tacit.   (Schön 1991, p. viii)

Quite simply, Schön argues, we cannot expect those in important areas of human endeavour to carry out their tasks without a place to reflect on what it is we are doing, how well we are doing it and how we might change and improve. Further, we need to learn in an appropriate way from the experience and wisdom of those who have been in ministry longer, as well as from our peers.

Review in this context will mean meeting regularly with others, not just to 'do business' but also to be reflective practitioners. Regular times of meeting (please, not Meetings!) of the church leadership to reflect and learn together will offer new insights, give support and encouragement, and help individuals to grow in faith.

Good practice, I believe, starts with the PCC not just having business meetings but also having such times of reflection, from away-days to a regular reflection slot on every business agenda.

But all involved in key ministry roles will need this time, too. In a smaller church it will mean the vicar spending time reflecting with the church organist or music leader, with the Sunday School leaders, with those leading pastoral care, with small-group or teaching leaders, etc. But it doesn't stop there: reflecting with the church treasurer, with those concerned with buildings and fabric, with fundraising and other practical issues, will pay huge dividends, as it will give context and meaning to their endeavours.

In larger churches, ensuring that regular meetings of pastoral teams, group leaders, staff, leadership and other teams have built-in and regular opportunities for reflection will be crucial to the life, vitality and mission perspective of each group.

The regular review which flows out of reflective practice will at best become a conscious part of every aspect of mission and ministry in a church, and will need to be seen as separate from (though integrated with) the important round of business meetings.

Reviewing mission and ministry

The final aspect of review will be the overarching and regular review of the mission and ministry imperatives of any church. As has already been discussed, there is a growing acceptance that every church should have a mission and ministry strategy. This will be specific to context and the life of the parish. The danger, though, with having such a strategy is that it can feel like a one-off exercise. So often, a Mission Action Plan or equivalent is a piece of paper which 'ticks the box' but is not a living document.

A meaningful mission and ministry strategy will be fully integrated with PCC agendas and with the whole life and mission of the church. As such it will not just be known and owned throughout the church, but will need to be regularly reviewed to ensure that it continues to reflect and set the priorities of the church. The same principles apply to reviewing mission and ministry as to reviewing individuals. There will need to be a clear background on which the review takes place: in this case a clearly defined strategy. Regular formal review will need to be built into the process. Again, this will show the value of SMART goals: where SMART goals have been set it will be easy to review progress and to adjust appropriately. And this will not necessarily need to wait for a formal annual or biennial review, but will be an on-going process.

The reality is, stuff happens! For example, a parish spends a great deal of time and energy preparing an excellent Mission

Action Plan which has SMART goals, is owned by the church community and is completely integrated with the decision-making process of the church. As a part of this process it is decided after much prayer and agonizing that although youth work is much needed the church simply doesn't have the resources to undertake the ministry. The Mission Action Plan therefore says that the strategy for youth work is to support the work of a neighbouring church in their endeavours. So far, so good. However, several weeks after the Mission Action Plan is agreed a couple start coming to church regularly and it transpires that not only are they qualified youth workers but they are keen to offer their services to the church. Clearly, the first reaction is not to say, 'Sorry, there is no way we can make this happen as it doesn't appear on our Mission Action Plan; you'll have to wait until the review in two years' time!' Immediate review and adjustment may well be appropriate.

In short, no plan, however good, should discount or block the promptings and movement of the Holy Spirit. Stuff happens, and constant review and appropriate adjustment can and should allow for this – not just in the major way illustrated here, but in minor ways such as new links developed, changes in income, movement in church membership and attendance.

And, of course, review will help a church to be confident in ending aspects of ministry and mission, in stopping activities, as well as in starting new projects, and in changing and adjusting existing initiatives. Just as with the difficult area of helping individuals to step down from ministries when appropriate, so ending established mission and ministry initiatives can be difficult when it becomes apparent that they are no longer fulfilling a useful purpose. People don't like letting their pet projects go. The great advantage of a built-in system of review is that it will establish objective criteria by which decisions can be made. This won't, of course, stop conflict arising, but it will be an important additional facet in discussion and decision-making processes.

Conclusion

Review and reflection can seem self-indulgent or burdensome, an activity which takes away time and energy from getting on with mission and ministry. However, when handled well and appropriately it will be life-enhancing and re-creational. So often mission and ministry initiatives can feel stale or 'more of the same'; good review processes are likely to give new life and energy to existing initiatives and to give space to new enterprise and challenge those areas which are past their sell-by date.

Similarly, the review process for individuals, and the encouragement towards reflective practice will allow space for the weary to step down or change direction and for the enthusiastic to find new vision and direction for their energies.

In all cases effective review can give objectivity, provide an environment to establish frameworks and criteria on which to base judgement and encourage a culture and context for creative change-management.

7

Why shared ministry?

All ministry stems from Christ and is corporate, belonging to the Church rather than the individual. The ordained, by their special concentration on and life-long commitment to exploring faith and discipleship, should be empowered to help others follow their own paths in these areas.

(Robin Greenwood 1994)

I clearly remember meeting the churchwardens of the church where I was to be vicar one dark and windy October evening at the back of a cold, draughty church. This was in the olden days before interview panels and application forms. The bishop said to this young curate, 'Such and such a church is vacant, why don't you take a look?' After telling the churchwardens about myself, I asked them what they would like of a new vicar. Their sole response was that he should visit old ladies and have cups of tea with them.

Behind the statement, it seemed to me, was a model (or caricature) of ordained ministry which, if it had ever really existed, was certainly long gone and was certainly not of 1980s inner-city London. As Martyn Percy writes:

In all kinds of informal conversations, one hears congregations muttering about the 'curate who used to visit everyone, all the time' ('those were the days'), or 'when the vicar baptized all-comers' ('the church was full then'). Not only is the past a foreign country, it is also the other side of the fence, where the grass was undoubtedly greener.   (Percy 2006)

In terms of pure logic, it is quite impossible for one vicar or even a small team of clergy to fulfil all the expectations of pastoral visiting, church leadership and management, worship preparation and sermon writing, teaching, mission and evangelism, community involvement, study and personal development that a romantic ideal of parish ministry might hold – and then say his or her prayers and have time for family, friends and self.

The reality of the massive culture change that has taken place in parish ministry following the move to the city with the Industrial Revolution, the effects of two world wars and the changed patterns of community, family and individual life has been recognized by the Church of England for many decades, with numerous reports being presented to General Synod and much being written about the need for a more active laity, increased lay ministry and the participation of all believers. The danger, it seems to me, though, is that we see lay ministry as plugging a gap left by declining numbers of stipendiary clergy and the increased pressures placed upon those remaining, rather than a theological imperative.

Robin Greenwood puts the changes that have been taking place succinctly, right back in 1994:

> In a typically unsung English Anglican manner, over the past decade, the bishops, General Synod, and their advisors have initiated a quiet but effective revolution ... The Church of England has been preparing for the dramatic change which is now coming about in the manner in which ministry is now offered both to church members and to the wider community.
>
> (Greenwood 1994, p. 55)

What I won't be doing in this chapter is rehearsing the well-worn theological arguments for the priesthood of all believers, for all-member ministry. I have little doubt that over the past 30 and more years this argument has prevailed throughout the Church of England – and in most other Christian traditions – and there are few, if any, clergy and regular church members who wouldn't agree with the principle.

The underlying issue that I would like to address here is the theological imperative that we are called to be in ministry together, in community, in relationship. It should never be a lone endeavour – either for the incumbent or for members of the congregation called or invited into particular ministries – but should always be a corporate undertaking.

A Trinitarian approach

The last quarter of the twentieth century saw, in theological writing and debate, a revival in the exploration of Trinitarian theology, from all traditions within the Church.[1] It was almost as if there was a recognition that various traditions had for too long been too strongly emphasizing one of the persons of the Godhead (to caricature, Catholics on the Fatherhood of God, Evangelicals on a personal relationship with Jesus and Charismatics on the gifts of the Holy Spirit).

Further, though, Greenwood (1994, pp. 77ff) suggests that for far too long Anglicans have been basing their models and patterns for ministry simply on the person of Jesus Christ: clergy as the successors of the Apostles, themselves appointed by Christ, with the gospel calling of sending out of disciples and the drawing new followers into the fellowship of Christ. There had been a tendency towards introspection, individualism and even separatism.

Greenwood's principal argument is that a reassessment of the doctrine of ministry and priesthood in the light of recent explorations in the doctrine of the Trinity points us firmly in the direction of a multi-faceted relational theology. We move, then, to a theology of priesthood which sees the Church not as separate from the world but as wholly a part of God's creation, and ministry not as separate and church-centred but rather as the Church's gift to the world. The focus of ministry becomes that of relationship, and that ministry sees the Church as wholly a part of the world, and in relationship with the world:

> For too long the Church has given the impression of being separate from rather than bound up in society. Uniquely, the Church has resources for fostering and nurturing communities of freedom and responsibility that testify to personal self-worth and imaginative creativity. Instead of distancing itself from the dilemmas of social institutions, the Church, recognizing itself as an institution, has the potential to demonstrate the beginnings of authentic sociality as 'an imaged response to the sociality of God'.   (Greenwood 1994, pp. 101–2)

Paul Fiddes' work on a pastoral doctrine of the Trinity (2000) clearly supports this approach. His arguments lead to a clear conclusion that Trinitarian theology points us emphatically to Christian living and pastoral ministry which can only be expressed in relationship and can be seen in terms of inter-dependency. In the life of the Trinity we see the ultimate mature relationship, based upon interdependence. We see a God who reveals himself as, and invites us to participate in, the blinding clarity of love, with all masks removed.

So, if we take it that ministry should be seen in the light of the relational theology of the life of the Trinity, it would seem natural and appropriate that priesthood and Christian ministry should be seen as essentially participative rather than individualistic. The term 'interdependency' is, I believe, crucial here. As discussed before, Jesus at the Ascension gives a clear mandate for mature discipleship; he sends the disciples out with full authority to make disciples, to baptize and to teach (Matthew 28.16–20). But he says that he is with them always. John reminds us that we are not comfortless, but that the Holy Spirit is with us (John 14.15–end). We are not inde-pendent, but neither are we dependent. We are called to mature relationships of interdependency within the Trinity and with one another.

Further, though, throughout the Gospels Jesus models ministry in relationship. He calls disciples who accompany him throughout his ministry; he sends disciples out in pairs. Even on the cross he commends his mother and his beloved disciple to one another.

This pattern of mature interdependency can be seen throughout the Bible. Take the example of Moses and Aaron, and then later Moses' father-in-law advising Moses to share leadership. The uncomfortable yet vital relationships between the kings of Israel and Judah and the prophets offer a fascinating study in interdependency. King David may well have found Nathan difficult and troublesome, but he would have been the first to admit that he couldn't have done without him. Throughout St Paul's writings we are left in no doubt of the many and various people who accompanied Paul on his travels and were a part of his endeavours. And the Acts of the Apostles gives us clear indications as to the dynamic of interdependency between the Apostles and the leadership of the early church – with its problems as well as its joys!

I would like, though, to offer one further model of interdependency which I have always found helpful in my ministry.

Wrestling Jacob

The same night [Jacob] got up and took his two wives, his two maids, and his eleven children, and crossed the ford of the Jabbok. He took them and sent them across the stream, and likewise everything that he had. Jacob was left alone; and a man wrestled with him until daybreak. When the man saw that he did not prevail against Jacob, he struck him on the hip socket; and Jacob's hip was put out of joint as he wrestled with him. Then he said, 'Let me go, for the day is breaking.' But Jacob said, 'I will not let you go, unless you bless me.' So he said to him, 'What is your name?' And he said, 'Jacob.' Then the man said, 'You shall no longer be called Jacob, but Israel, for you have striven with God and with humans, and have prevailed.' Then Jacob asked him,

'Please tell me your name.' But he said, 'Why is it that you ask my name?' And there he blessed him. So Jacob called the place Peniel, saying, 'For I have seen God face to face, and yet my life is preserved.' The sun rose upon him as he passed Penuel, limping because of his hip. (Genesis 32.22–31)

Jacob, through his early craftiness with his brother, his flourishing against the odds with his uncle and his learning to walk in the ways of God, has reached a turning point in his life. He is about to confront his past by meeting his brother Esau, and has taken up the reins of the full authority of leadership for his family, which has become a tribe.

We meet Jacob in this passage wrestling with God. Jacob, who has reached maturity in his relationships and is confronting the conflicts and difficulties in his life, wrestles with God. He neither submits nor does he try to press home advantage. The importance of this story is in the wrestling, not in the winning or losing. And, further, Jacob carries the mark of the wrestling into the next stage of his journey, the meeting with Esau.

I find this a powerful story because it expresses something of the interdependency that God, in his infinite generosity, offers to his people. Not only is Jacob made aware of his dependency on God, but God allows for his dependency on his chosen servant. In the wrestling he names Jacob Israel and calls him to be the father of his chosen people; God is dependent upon Jacob. Although, ultimately, the balance is unequal with an all-powerful God dealing with a frail human, God in his infinite love and trust ensures that in this wrestling begins a relationship of interdependence, which continues throughout the Bible, through the Incarnation, and throughout the history of humankind, from the perspective of faith.

But this relationship of interdependence is clearly costly, and is symbolized by 'the man' having to plead with Jacob to let him go and Jacob receiving a dislocated hip.

Interdependence is a vital ingredient in all our dealings in faith; it is of its essence about mature relationships. It can be seen in Jesus' letting go at the Ascension, in the relationship of the Trinity in which we are called to participate. It is modelled and seen in the mature relationship of grown-up children and parents. It is for this reason that we look to the terminology of Father and Son when we think of the first two persons of the Trinity; in the relationship of Father and Son we find the fully mature interdependent parent–child relationship. And this is the relationship that we are called to as Christians with the Godhead.

But, like all child–parent relationships, maturity only develops through the process of wrestling and we carry the marks of that wrestling throughout our lives.

Practical implications

In practical terms, what this means is that in all expressions of Christian ministry we should not expect to go it alone, and neither should we expect others to do so. At its worst, some theological colleges in former years unconsciously taught and encouraged those preparing for ordination to be (a caricature of) a pope in their parish. They prepared them for a lonely ministry, without friendship in their parish and effectively undertaking all aspects of ministry themselves. Not only was this an unhelpful and untheological model, it was also a recipe for arrogance and eventually for burn-out.

In recent years there has been great encouragement across the Church of England for parishes to develop Ministry Leadership Teams. In principle I wholeheartedly welcome this move, though regret that the initiatives have often come about through the perception of organizational necessity rather than through sound theological imperative. We do it because we need to co-opt others into running an increasingly complex parish situation (multi-parish benefices, perhaps, and too much for one person to do), rather than because it is modelling the good practice seen in Scriptures, in the Gospels and life of Jesus, and in the practice of the early church (and commonly in the medieval church).

Ministry Leadership Teams

Once again, Ministry Leadership Teams can be a mechanistic response to a perceived problem or they can develop and grow organically. We have the following jobs to be done/services to take/sermons to preach/people to visit, etc.; who can we co-opt to fill the gaps? Rather than looking at how to fill the gaps or how to keep the show on the road, when considering the development of a Ministry Leadership Team the questions to ask are, 'What sort of ministry is God calling us to in this place?' and 'Who has God sent us?' Growing a Ministry Leadership Team from this perspective will then be much more of a corporate venture under God, and will be built on the firm foundations of relationships, with one another and with God.

An effective and fruitful Ministry Leadership Team will grow and develop organically; will involve wrestling, reflection and developing relationships; and will be relevant and appropriate to context. There is no blue-print, no one-size-fits-all to Ministry Leadership Teams and their development. However, inviting a consultant to assist in the developmental process may offer an objectivity as a Ministry Leadership Team develops.

Conclusion

In Christian ministry, then, we will not be looking so much for a hierarchical structure within which to place ministries, but rather the building of ministerial relationships based on interdependency. No one, from senior bishop or pastor through highly skilled psychotherapist or counsellor to experienced and loving parent or carer, will have all the answers for Christian ministry. But in acknowledging and using the skills, experience and wisdom of one another, within the love and embrace of the Trinity, we can seek through interdependence to address the needs and concerns of our ministries and the people we encounter. And indeed, those we encounter will, too, become a part of that interdependency.

8

An integrated and structured approach

> It is not enough, in other words, that those called to the ministry refrain from or do certain things; it is necessary that they be the kind of persons, that they have the character, to sustain them in ministry ... It is not enough that a person is not 'immoral' neither should they be vain, proud, intemperate, cowardly, ingratiating, and unloving. Moreover, it must be asked whether a person exhibits the patience and hope so necessary to the ministry. For without patience and hope there is little chance a person will have the constancy to sustain him or her through the disappointments and betrayals so often involved in the ministry.   (Stanley Hauerwas 1988, p. 135)[1]

And it is simply not enough to find a 'good person' and appoint that person to a ministry and expect him or her to get on with it. What I am arguing for in this book is the growing of a whole culture of development: a culture which will expect people to want to develop in their Christian discipleship, and a culture in which those who are in places and positions of Christian ministry will expect to receive and encounter training, education and formation for ministry, both at the initial stages and on a continuing basis.

In this chapter I shall offer a variety of perspectives of what a culture of development will look like and will include.

Process and content

Any event in a parish aimed at ministry development (indeed, any parish activity) will contain a mixture of process and content; the two can usually be divided fairly clearly, although there will be grey areas where the two blend. This will be true on a surface, at semi-hidden and at deeply hidden levels. A simple illustration would be a group of people who are spending a series of evenings studying St John's Gospel. The content will be the Gospel, commentaries and accompanying texts, their experience of applying the Gospel, etc. The process will include how the evening is structured, where they meet, what they do about refreshments, the number of people in the group, ground rules for the sessions (implicit or explicit), and so on. A 'grey area' might be a decision to invite a biblical scholar to lead one or more of the sessions; in doing so his or her presence will influence both content (in bringing the scholar's own slant on the material) and process (in offering a particular way of leading the event; indeed, this person's presence will offer a dynamic to the group which would not have otherwise been present).

For members of the group to say, 'But we just want to study St John's Gospel, we don't care about how we do it,' would be to seriously underestimate the importance of process. The process will have a major impact on the content of the sessions (and vice versa). For example, if one person is allowed to dominate the discussion a very different outcome is likely to pertain than if each person is given equal opportunity to contribute. Similarly, a group of six people will have a very different type of discussion from a group of 30 people. More subtly, however, a difficult journey to the venue or cold coffee on arrival can have a greater influence on a session than an ill-prepared speaker.

In the same way, a dense, inaccessible or irrelevant presentation, however scholarly, can leave participants feeling that they have wasted their evening, even if the content could be 'shown' to be of the highest academic quality.

One of my own areas of concern in offering training for clergy, laity and parish groups is the importance of group dynamics in church activities. As we have explored, the Christian faith is supremely relational. I passionately believe that if we cannot create an appropriate environment for learning and developing, then all our endeavours can be wasted or even counter-productive.

Process

To underline the importance of good process for developing in Christian ministry, I begin this section with a 'story meditation' from the 'Education' section of Anthony de Mello's *The Heart of the Enlightened* (1997).

> A man began to give large doses of cod-liver oil to his Doberman because he had been told that the stuff was good for dogs. Each day he would hold the head of the protesting dog between his knees, force its jaws open, and pour the liquid down its throat.
>
> One day the dog broke loose and spilled the oil on the floor. Then, to the man's great surprise, it returned to lick the spoon. That is when he discovered that what the dog had been fighting was not the oil, but his method of administering it.

In research I have undertaken on training and development programmes I have run for clergy,[2] a number of clear themes have consistently been identified as contributing to the effectiveness of the programmes offered. Perhaps surprisingly, a significant aspect of these themes is that they are all either wholly or in large part related to process rather than content.

Interviewees were asked to identify a range of words to describe the positive attributes of the programmes. The following were the most commonly used:

- collaborative
- supportive
- challenging
- accountable
- reflective
- conducive
- creative
- re-creative

- affirming
- formative
- contextual
- attractive
- self-motivating
- change-orientated
- culturally relevant.

However, not only are the themes substantially process-orientated, but they are also substantially relationship-orientated. This is hardly surprising if we accept that the Christian faith is, at its heart, relational. In development provision, then, relational issues play a large part in defining what makes for a good and fruitful experience.

In the Christian faith we look to Jesus as the archetypal teacher, and we see in the Gospels Jesus teaching his disciples in small groups (three or 12) and in larger groups (sometimes 5,000 or more). But it is in the building of relationship that the best learning takes place; we find Jesus with his disciples involved in their formation from disciples to Apostles, developing their skills of teaching, preaching and healing and educating them in interpreting the Scriptures in the context of the kingdom that Jesus comes to preach. This relational model is underpinned by the Incarnation, the Word made flesh who comes among us, 'full of grace and truth' (John 1.14). Our God is not a distant God, but a God who comes to us in human flesh and sends the Holy Spirit to be with us always, a God who promises not a set of rules from which to govern our lives but a living relationship which he calls on us to live and sustain.

In the same way, throughout its history Christianity has always been, and continues to be, expressed in community. Doctrines have been developed and teaching takes place in the context of the Church of Jesus Christ, in its many expressions. Teaching and learning is a corporate, relational enterprise. Today, as Bob Jackson clearly demonstrates,[3] the churches which are growing are those with organized discipleship and nurture programmes. One of the common features of courses (such as Alpha, Emmaus, etc.) is the relational aspect of the teaching and learning; learning takes place in groups where individuals build up relationships with one another and with those leading the programme. The Alpha Supper is now a characteristic feature of this programme. It is no coincidence that Jesus is often reported in the Gospels as sharing meals with those among whom he is making his disciples and followers.

The relational nature of the teaching and learning process is, of course, not unique to the Christian faith. In his introduction to the professional development of teachers, Philip Adey reminds us that:

> it is not an historical accident, nor throw-back to medieval practice, nor the hopeless inertia of the system that has led to all school education, everywhere in the world, to be conducted in 'classes' of from 15 to 90 students with one 'teacher'.
>
> (Adey 2004, p. 3)

Similarly all good adult education practice in colleges, universities and courses has tutorial, seminar and learning groups at the centre of the teaching and learning experience. It seems beyond doubt that a high priority for process in developing Christians in ministry will be, then, that it is relational.

A structured approach to development

To synthesize these various perspectives on the process of ministry development, I now offer a process structure which I believe is applicable to all Christian training, education and development. The structure is at its heart organic in approach, and speaks to a culture which begins with the question, 'Why wouldn't you want to be a part of this?' rather than the statement, 'You ought to be doing this.'

Although interpretation will be required, it will be applicable to all church-based provision. It offers the relational approach which I believe is at the heart of all fruitful development. It could, of course, be seen simply as organized common sense, but this is in its favour, for although it is supported by research and educational theory, it will also be simple and straightforward to apply.

As an important reference point for this section, it would be useful to bear in mind Abraham Maslow's acclaimed 'Hierarchy of Needs'.[4] The process laid out below can be seen alongside the framework of this pyramid, which sees physical and safety (boundary) needs as a given before other developmental needs can be fulfilled. Each of these stages can be found within this process.

Preparation

Before any event is undertaken a simple issue should be addressed: 'Is this really necessary? What is the evidence to support using time, energy and resources in this way?' The huge danger is that we lay on something simply because we know someone who has an expertise in this field, or it's the latest thing, or it's my personal hobby-horse, or the last conversation that some bishop or other has had with someone, or something is better than nothing, or it worked in another parish . . . It is essential that development provision addresses the needs of the individuals at whom it is targeted and/or the needs of the church (and where the latter, careful consideration needs to be given as to how these needs can be addressed in such a way that they can be seen in the context of the individual and his or her situation).

Once the need has been established, a methodology should be defined which will include such factors as duration, venue, resources and budget, target audience, optimum (with maximum and minimum) numbers, learning styles, leaders and speakers.

Invitation

I have deliberately used the word 'invitation' here, rather than the more commonly used word 'publicity'. My experience both as a parish priest and as a clergy development practitioner is that publicity applies to other people! However professional and attractive general publicity may seem, the likelihood is that busy people will give it a cursory glance and unless it fulfils a pressing need or interest it will head for the bin. A clearly focused and personal invitation, however, is multi-beneficial. In the first case, well worded, it is likely to be affirming to the recipient, whether or not that person attends ('I've been noticed'), and this might well emanate from the incumbent. Second, it ensures that the target audience is being personally addressed, and third, it expects a response, and can easily be followed up if no response is received. (The invitational approach may well be accompanied by a general release, depending on the nature of the event; this may ensure that no one feels excluded, while realistically expecting little or no response.)

The invitation can be the pivotal point of an event; it can set the whole tone for a particular development venture. Positively, if participants feel that the event is helpful and that they are a valued part of the event from the first contact, this will be hugely beneficial to the whole process. Conversely, if worded badly an invitation can have a seriously deleterious effect. One five-day clergy residential event which I organized included an initial invitation sent out by bishops. As a result of inadequate communication between myself and one of the bishops concerned, the invitation he sent out left some of the invitees with the sense that their arms were being twisted to attend. The result was that three participants arrived at a five-day residential highly resentful. A tried and trusted residential programme, which had run successfully on numerous previous occasions, was spoiled by these three, to the detriment of all attending, including the staff.

However, this unfortunate experience gave (at least) three important learning outcomes. First, there was the recognition that people will always bring their own personal agendas to any event. It will be vital to draw these out right at the beginning of the event. Second, we reviewed the way in which we prepared people for the programme, ensuring (in this case through a pre-course meeting) that each was as clear as possible not just about the course itself but also about why he or she had been invited to attend.

The third learning outcome leads directly on to the next issue in terms of process, and concerns venue. Because of an error at the conference venue we were allocated the wrong room for our first session. This meant that the staff were thrown by using an unfamiliar and inappropriate setting, seating 16 people so that they could not see each other properly and in deep armchairs directly after lunch. It was therefore possible for one of the dissidents to opt out of the introductory session. Further, the audio-visual equipment was not accessible to all those in the room. The event got off to a dreadful start, and the staff battled to 'hold' the course from there on.

Venue

The venue for an event, then, can prove to be the single most important factor in participants' engagement – or otherwise – in the event. The above unfortunate example demonstrates how easily this can go wrong. A good venue can, however, have a transforming effect on the way in which participants receive training and development. Selecting an appropriate venue to accompany a particular event can prove crucial, and ensuring that a positive ambience greets participants on arrival will inevitably begin an event with those attending in a positive frame of mind to participate.

Alongside the physical environment is the important issue of meals and refreshments. Again, when participants' needs are taken seriously, as Maslow suggests, they will be free for developmental considerations. Further, though, where hospitality is taken as a serious integral part of the process it will provide a positive background ambience which will greatly enhance the learning environment.

The training and education presentational process

The process of presentation is a complex mix of a number of factors, which require skills and time to balance appropriately. Skill and experience in planning a programme for any event, from a single evening to a course or a weekend away, is vital for anyone involved in delivering training and development.

Elements will include a well-balanced programme which importantly provides proper breaks (and in whole day or longer events, free time for conversation, networking or to have space). Presentation and teaching sessions will take learning styles seriously, acknowledging the reality that people have varying learning-style preferences and taking into account the various processes involved in learning.[5]

Contextual relevance will be an important ingredient in the learning process. Participants should be able to readily identify themselves and their contexts in material presented; in other words, it should be relevant to them in their own lives. Ideally participants may be asked to contribute something of their own experience to the process, as this will offer a higher degree of involvement and ownership, while offering an important 'cross-reference' to those presenting and leading that they are connecting with the audience.

Developing this last point, I would argue that the best training and development is led and presented by those who can be flexible and responsive to their audience. Not only will this mean that presentations are most relevant to the situations of those present, but it is also likely to increase the engagement of participants if they feel that they are serious partners in the learning process.

Other factors to be taken into account include training and education being inclusive rather than divisive, and elements which are experiential and creative and, hopefully, some fun!

Space

The temptation when gathering a group together is to pack a programme as full as possible so that a great deal can be conveyed. Simple common sense tells us that we need time to assimilate information; inadequate space to reflect and to interact is likely to lead to a poor learning experience, yet so often that simple factor is forgotten.

It is often said, jokingly, that the best clergy training and development takes place in the bar. However, the space symbolized by 'the bar' is a crucial element in any well-organized event. The provision of appropriate spaces for social interaction between participants, and with leaders offers not only a levelling experience but the opportunity to meet with one another as human beings. Such space will offer opportunities for those who would not normally encounter one another to interact, and for opportunity to share experience and exchange stories, as well as assimilate and discuss the learning taking place.

A lack of relationship building can develop the tendency for individuals to entrench and build fortresses around their opinions and stances. I would argue that training and development offers an ideal and rigorous opportunity, in a safe and conducive environment, for participants to open their hearts and minds to others, to challenge and be challenged, without being too threatened. On many occasions I have witnessed clergy colleagues of wildly differing church traditions rationally discussing controversial and challenging issues over a meal at a clergy training event, where in their local situations they would have avoided one another. Well-executed events can provide vital safe territory where even in the most cohesive of congregations opinions and standpoints can differ wildly.

Affirmation and challenge

In our Christian journey these two elements can be vital, but in the normal run of life easily overlooked. So often Christians can feel isolated in their work, in their neighbourhoods or in their day-to-day lives. Participation in training and development events should offer an important opportunity for people to feel affirmed in their faith and, in meeting with others on a similar journey, for them to feel that others face similar issues.

However, it will also be important that participants are made to feel challenged. If everything is too comfortable there will be no place for growth. As we've already seen, wrestling with issues is a necessary part of developing as Christians. Further, there is a danger that people can be left with half-understood truths and unchallenged prejudices if they are not exposed to rigour in a development process.

Next steps and follow-up

In bringing an event to an end there will be appropriate closure, but at the same time giving the possibilities for next steps in continuing development. A one-off half-day on, say, bereavement visiting will have a very different conclusion from a regular Bible study group or a weekend exploring the Church's healing ministry. But each will have clear endings and follow-up, whether it's further reading, where to go for further information or who are the local reference points. For more substantial courses further support or contact may well be appropriate (such as follow-up meetings for a group which has shared deeply over a number of weeks, or on-going support for those in a new ministry).

However, with next steps, follow-up and endings, clarity is essential, with those delivering the events not offering more than they are able to deliver.

This stage of the process will also include an appropriate method of evaluation, so that the provision itself can be continually a learning and developing process and so that participants can see that they are a continuing part of the process and that their input and response is of value.

As can be seen, those involved in the delivery of training and development will have many balls to juggle in order that the process takes place effectively, fruitfully and beneficially for all involved, and that the resources of time, money and talents are best used in providing opportunities that enhance both the lives and ministries of participants and the needs and objectives of the Church. However, those who take process seriously will also be taking the organic approach seriously; it is in the establishment of good and appropriate process that the door can be held wide open for participants to find and achieve the greatest benefit in terms of ownership and learning outcomes for their own situations.

Conclusion

When I was at theological college the constant refrain of my pastoral studies tutor was, 'Time spent with people is never wasted.' On one level I have always thought this to be complete rubbish; I have lost count of the hours absorbed in ministry by time-wasters, the self-obsessed and those who think the parish priest's time should be wholly devoted to them. However, behind this comment there is, I believe, a profound truth (and hopefully what my pastoral studies tutor was getting at!). At its heart our faith is relational, and it is in developing relationships appropriately that ministry development begins. This is at the core of the organic model for which I am arguing in this book.

Ultimately, the organic model of ministry development is one of developing relationships so that individuals, congregations and communities can discern the best and most appropriate ways of developing, and thus take responsibility for their own development, under God.

The great joy and blessing of the Church of England is the richness of varied church traditions and the differing character of churches across the country. There is clearly no one 'right' way of being Church; nor can there ever be.

The danger is that we fall into an institutionalized approach as clergy, as Christians, as Church: a way of thinking which suggests there is only one 'right' way – whether it's for PCC agendas, for Sunday liturgy and worship, for training and development, or for organizing pastoral ministry. The reality, I argue, must entail responding to the particular context and exploring the people and the factors that are current: who and what has God given us? It is imperative that ministry and ministry development initiatives are shaped and adapted to what is appropriate for us, now, here. Just because it worked in my last parish, in the big parish down the road or at the conference I've just attended, in the book I've just read, doesn't mean it can be adopted wholesale to a new situation.

Effective ministry development will require constant change and adaptation as we are called to respond to the people, cultures and new situations that God is constantly surprising us with. Such is the joy and the challenge of being involved in developing ministry.

There are many and various resources available to assist in this process of exploration, but none will be 'just right' for any individual situation. Being organic rather that mechanistic in approach will require imagination and an artistic touch, alongside analysis and systematic implementation.

Importantly, though, it should never be a lone venture. Within a parish situation there will need to be those who journey together and it will be important to find ways of discovering approaches that are appropriate theologically, culturally and practically.

Developing ministry organically clearly suggests a dynamic approach. Such an approach is, particularly in the initial stages, much more work and more time-consuming. The process entails naming and exploring the prevalent culture, examining and exploring background features to the given situation and spending time in developing relationships. It will require clear identification of the skills, passions and gifts of those God sends us as co-workers in ministry and the exploration of the dynamics of the groups in which we are involved.

Further, the approach will require coaching and supporting those in ministry, organized reflection and review and time spent in ensuring good preparation for any event or initiative. All of this sounds a heavy burden, particularly if you just want to get on with it (just do it?). And yes, there is clearly a danger that all this focusing on organic development means that nothing actually gets achieved.

It is, of course, a balance, which is why I am clear that using techniques such as SMART objectives ensures that clear forward motion is achieved. I am convinced, though, that time spent in developing ministry organically will pay huge dividends in all aspects of parish life and in preaching the good news of Jesus Christ. In the long term it will provide firm foundations. It will establish a culture where mission initiatives, discipleship and pastoral care can flourish. It will enable individuals to feel valued, have ownership and see themselves as fully a part of the mission and ministry of God's Church in their local situation and in building the kingdom of God.

Appendix 1

Who cares? A Lent course designed for All Hallows Church, Twickenham

Introduction

This course was especially written for All Hallows Church to help the church think together about the gospel imperatives of caring for one another, and to explore how we might best carry these out for their church today. As a result of the course a pastoral care team with 12 members has been trained and set up in the parish.

The word 'pastoral' comes from the Latin *pastor*, meaning 'shepherd', and refers to the biblical idea of one who looks after others as caring for them as a shepherd cares for his or her sheep. In pastoral care we look towards Jesus as our example – the Good Shepherd.

Practical issues

Each session of the course will follow the same structure. All timings will be approximate, but no session should last more than an hour and a half.

At the beginning of the course, when the group meets for the first time, the group may like to set some **ground rules**. These might include such things as confidentiality, agreeing to listen to one another and starting and ending on time. These will vary from group to group.

There are many questions posed during the course. There are no 'right' and 'wrong' answers to these; they are asked in order to help us think about the subject from a variety of perspectives. Not all questions have to be covered (it's not an exam!).

Finally, there is no need to get through every bit of the course; the leader will guide the group and if at the end of the session you haven't got through all the material, it really doesn't matter (you can always carry on at home!).

Structure of the sessions

Prayer (5 mins)

Each session begins with a time of quiet and prayer. It will be up to each group to decide how best to use this time – it might include a formal prayer, a time of silence or a prayer led by a different member of the group each week. A candle may be lit and placed in the centre of the group.

Introduction (5 mins)

The group leader introduces the aims of the session and ensures that everyone understands and is comfortable with what is intended of the session.

Bible study (15 mins)

A passage (or passages) from the Bible will begin to set the scene for the session. The passage(s) will be read aloud and then there will be a brief pause for everyone to digest it. Group members will then be asked to reflect on what the passage says to them.

Commentary (10 mins)

The group leader will introduce a short commentary, which will help to explore the theme. Members will then be invited to respond, expressing what this says to them.

Experience (15 mins)

Group members will then be invited to share, from their own experience, things that help to say something to the theme of the session, giving further elucidation.

Questions (15 mins)

There will be a number of questions for the group to discuss and respond to with their own thoughts and opinions, in the light of the previous discussions. The group may like to divide into pairs or smaller groups for this.

Conclusion (5 mins)

The group leader will sum up the session, pointing to important themes that members may like to take away for their thoughts and prayers during the week.

Prayer (5 mins)

The session will end with a time of prayer (see above). This may include a time for members to express their own prayers aloud. You may like to use the following prayer in your sessions or in your own prayers:

> Christ has no body now on earth but ours,
>   no hands but ours, no feet but ours.
> Ours are the eyes through which
> must look out Christ's compassion on the world.
> Ours are the feet with which
> he is to go about doing good.
> Ours are the hands with which
> he is to bless people now.
> Amen.
>
>   (St Teresa of Avila, adapted)

Week 1
Pastoral care and the Bible

Prayer (5 mins)

Introduction (5 mins)

The aim of this session is to explore what the Bible has to tell us about caring for one another.

Bible study (15 mins)

Moses' father-in-law said to him, 'What you are doing is not good. You will surely wear yourself out, both you and these people with you. For the task is too heavy for you; you cannot do it alone. Now listen to me. I will give you counsel, and God be with you! You should represent the people before God, and you should bring their cases before God; teach them the statutes and instructions and make known to them the way they are to go and the things they are to do. You should also look for able men among all the people, men who fear God, are trustworthy, and hate dishonest gain; set such men over them as officers over thousands, hundreds, fifties and tens. Let them sit as judges for the people at all times; let them bring every important case to you, but decide every minor case themselves. So it will be easier for you, and they will bear the burden with you. If you do this, and God so commands you, then you will be able to endure, and all these people will go to their home in peace.' So Moses listened to his father-in-law and did all that he had said.

(Exodus 18.17–24)

But be doers of the word, and not merely hearers who deceive themselves. For if any are hearers of the word and not doers, they are like those who look at themselves in a mirror; for they look at themselves and, on going away, immediately forget what they were like. But those who look into the perfect law, the law of liberty, and persevere, being not hearers who forget but doers who act – they will be blessed in their doing. If any think they are religious, and do not bridle their tongues but deceive their hearts, their religion is worthless. Religion that is pure and undefiled before God, the Father, is this: to care for orphans and widows in their distress, and to keep oneself unstained by the world. (James 1.22–27)

- How do you think the people of Israel felt before and after Moses' father-in-law's advice was carried out?
- What might be the situation in the church that James is writing to?
- Can you think of other Bible passages which talk of people caring for and about one another?

Commentary (10 mins)

Even from the cross, Jesus was concerned for the people around him. In the midst of his agony he showed compassion and reached out in love. He spoke and listened to those who were crucified beside him, and promised forgiveness and eternal life to one. Jesus called on John to take his mother into his own home.

- What other examples can you think of, where Jesus showed care and compassion for others?

Experience (15 mins)

Now share some of your own experiences, from those you know – first hand – who care for others. Do they do this from a position of faith?

Questions (15 mins)

- Is there anything unique in the Christian faith that calls us to care for others?
- Are we called to care just for other Christians – or even first for other Christians?
- What does the image of Jesus the Good Shepherd have to say to us?

Conclusion (5 mins)

Prayer (5 mins)

Week 2
Pastoral care and the Church

Prayer (5 mins)

Introduction (5 mins)

The aim of this session is to reflect together on what pastoral care means in the context of the Church, both historically and today.

Bible study (15 mins)

I am the good shepherd. The good shepherd lays down his life for the sheep. The hired hand, who is not the shepherd and does not own the sheep, sees the wolf coming and leaves the sheep and runs away – and the wolf snatches them and scatters them. The hired hand runs away because a hired hand does not care for the sheep. I am the good shepherd. I know my own and my own know me, just as the Father knows me and I know the Father. And I lay down my life for the sheep. I have other sheep that do not belong to this fold. I must bring them also, and they will listen to my voice. So there will be one flock, one shepherd.   (John 10.11–16)

- Jesus spoke to the experience of his listeners. What do you think it was like to be a shepherd in first-century Palestine?
- If Jesus was speaking to an audience today, what image might he have used instead of shepherd?
- What feelings does the image of Jesus, the Good Shepherd, stir up inside me?

Commentary (10 mins)

Even from the early times the Church was involved in looking for practical ways of showing its care for others. In the Acts of the Apostles and in St Paul's letters we hear of the general distribution to those in need.

The Christian Church began schools and hospitals. The earliest recorded school in Britain is King's School, Canterbury, founded in 597 as a part of St Augustine's mission. St Bartholomew's Hospital in the City of London was founded in 1123 by the monk Rahere. Missionary activity frequently includes the establishment of such institutions. Religious communities have always put hospitality high on their priorities. In recent times the Church has pioneered the hospice movement.

- Can you think of other examples of the ways in which the Church as an institution (as opposed to individual Christians) has been involved in pastoral care?

Experience (15 mins)

From your experience, does it make any real difference if an institution has a Christian foundation?

Questions (15 mins)

- It takes time and money for the Church to be involved in schools, hospitals and other institutions. Do you think that this is good stewardship of limited resources?
- Jesus sent his disciples out to 'Go and make disciples of all nations . . .' Does the Church's involvement in institutions fulfil this Great Commission?
- Psalm 23 talks of the shepherd as one who 'leads me forth beside the waters of comfort' (BCP). Does the imagery of this psalm have anything to say to us in this situation?

Conclusion (5 mins)

Prayer (5 mins)

Week 3
What does it mean to care?

Prayer (5 mins)

Introduction (5 mins)

The aim of this session is to consider the priority that care for others has for us, in our Christian journey.

Bible study (15 mins)

Now the whole group of those who believed were of one heart and soul, and no one claimed private ownership of any possessions, but everything they owned was held in common. With great power the apostles gave their testimony to the resurrection of the Lord Jesus, and great grace was upon them all. There was not a needy person among them, for as many as owned lands or houses sold them and brought the proceeds of what was sold. They laid it at the apostles' feet, and it was distributed to each as any had need. There was a Levite, a native of Cyprus, Joseph, to whom the apostles gave the name Barnabas (which means 'son of encouragement'). He sold a field that belonged to him, then brought the money, and laid it at the apostles' feet. (Acts 4.32–37)

- In what ways would you say this passage expresses what it means to care for one another?
- How might we be called to be sacrificial in our care of others?
- In what ways is living a life of care for others a missionary activity?

Commentary (10 mins)

In Christian pastoral care, the carers work within a framework that has as its basis the belief that all people are made in the image and likeness of God (Genesis 1.27–28). Therefore, pastoral care can be seen as involvement in the caring response of God to humanity, humanity to humanity, and humanity to God (Luke 10.27). Pastoral care, then, is seen in the context of the whole work of God. The task will involve skill, prayer and reflection in uncovering what will be the best response to any given situation.

- Does this make Christian pastoral care different or distinctive from the rest of the world? In what ways?

Experience (15 mins)

- Who are the people you look to as following in the footsteps of Jesus in caring for the wounded, hurt and broken in our world?

Questions (15 mins)

- Some people are more difficult for us to like than others, if we're honest. How do we cope with caring for and about our noisy, nosey or rude neighbour?
- Jesus not only cared for people at the bottom of the heap, he also ate with them and shared his life with them. To what extent should we be involved in the lives of others?
- Shepherds lived dirty, dangerous and lonely lives. How does the image of the shepherd (pastor) stand up for us in our caring for others?

Conclusion (5 mins)

Prayer (5 mins)

Week 4
Pastoral care in our everyday lives

Prayer (5 mins)

Introduction (5 mins)

The aim of this session is to consider in what ways we can and do care for others.

Bible study (15 mins)

Just then a lawyer stood up to test Jesus. 'Teacher,' he said, 'what must I do to inherit eternal life?' He said to him, 'What is written in the law? What do you read there?' He answered, 'You shall love the Lord your God with all your heart, and with all your soul, and with all your strength, and with all your mind; and your neighbour as yourself.' And he said to him, 'You have given the right answer; do this, and you will live.' But wanting to justify himself, he asked Jesus, 'And who is my neighbour?' Jesus replied, 'A man was going down from Jerusalem to Jericho, and fell into the hands of robbers, who stripped him, beat him, and went away, leaving him half dead. Now by chance a priest was going down that road; and when he saw him, he passed by on the other side. So likewise a Levite, when he came to the place and saw him, passed by on the other side. But a Samaritan while travelling came near him; and when he saw him, he was moved with pity. He went to him and bandaged his wounds, having poured oil and wine on them. Then he put him on his own animal, brought him to an inn, and took care of him. The next day he took out two denarii, gave them to the innkeeper, and said, "Take care of him; and when I come back, I will repay you whatever more you spend." Which of these three, do you think, was a neighbour to the man who fell into the hands of the robbers?' He said, 'The one who showed him mercy.' Jesus said to him, 'Go and do likewise.'   (Luke 10.25–37)

- Which person in this passage do you most relate to?
- How do you think the lawyer felt? Was it easy for him to 'Go and do likewise'?
- Sin might be described as failure to love God, neighbour and self. What is your reaction to such a description?

Commentary (10 mins)

Henri Nouwen, a famous Christian writer and pastor, wrote a book called *The Wounded Healer*, which speaks of his own experience of brokenness, being cared for and caring for others. It does seem to be that often (though by no means always) those who are among the best healers and carers are those who have been through major problems, hurt and illness in their own lives – and have worked through it. For example, many Relate counsellors (marriage guidance) have had broken marriages.

- What effect has pain and hurt in your own life had on your attitude towards care of others?

Experience (15 mins)

Share together some times in your own life when you have found it easy and when you have found it difficult to care for someone else.

Questions (15 mins)

- What are modern equivalents of 'passing by on the other side of the road'? Have you ever done so?
- What is the relationship between the things that you do for others and Christian mission and witness?
- What is your favourite image or picture of caring for others? (It might be biblical, artistic or drawn from life.)

Conclusion (5 mins)

Prayer (5 mins)

Week 5
Pastoral care and us

Prayer (5 mins)

Introduction (5 mins)

The aim of this session is to draw together our thoughts and discussions over the past weeks, and draw out the implications for our own church as a caring Christian community.

Bible study (15 mins)

Jesus, knowing that the Father had given all things into his hands, and that he had come from God and was going to God, got up from the table, took off his outer robe, and tied a towel around himself. Then he poured water into a basin and began to wash the disciples' feet and to wipe them with the towel that was tied around him. He came to Simon Peter, who said to him, 'Lord, are you going to wash my feet?' Jesus answered, 'You do not know now what I am doing, but later you will understand.' Peter said to him, 'You will never wash my feet.' Jesus answered, 'Unless I wash you, you have no share with me.' Simon Peter said to him, 'Lord, not my feet only but also my hands and my head!' Jesus said to him, 'One who has bathed does not need to wash, except for the feet, but is entirely clean. And you are clean, though not all of you.' For he knew who was to betray him; for this reason he said, 'Not all of you are clean.' After he had washed their feet, had put on his robe, and had returned to the table, he said to them, 'Do you know what I have done to you? You call me Teacher and Lord – and you are right, for that is what I am. So if I, your Lord and Teacher, have washed your feet, you also ought to wash one another's feet. For I have set you an example, that you also should do as I have done to you.'   (John 13.3–15)

• Washing feet was the job of the lowest servant. How do you think Peter and the rest of the disciples felt when Jesus washed their feet?

- What would you say is the modern equivalent of washing one another's feet?
- How do we respond to the image of Jesus, the Servant King?

Commentary (10 mins)

We probably all have an image of a rural idyll for a settled village community, with its own church and vicar, a pub, a post office and a shop, a doctor and local midwife – and everybody knows each other, cares for each other – and knows each other's business! Such communities hardly exist today, and probably not in our locality. Lives have become much more complex, people work longer hours and live more private lives. They travel far more easily, and often don't know their neighbours.

We might regret the passing of such communities, but it is a reality that life has changed. Following Jesus' command, though, it is still at the heart of the gospel to care for one another.

- In what ways might we encourage our local community to be more caring of one another?

Experience (15 mins)

The rural idyll was not, of course, as romantic as the myth would have us believe. One of the down sides was that it was a busybody's paradise; what could pass for 'caring' might in fact be simple nosiness and gossip. Share together ways in which caring might go wrong – or has gone wrong for you.

Questions (15 mins)

- Who would you say is called to be a carer in our community?
- How might we organize ourselves at our own church to ensure that everyone is cared for?
- Has your understanding of the image of Jesus the Good Shepherd changed or developed over the past weeks?

Conclusion (5 mins)

Prayer (5 mins)

About the course

The course was written for Lent groups taking place at All Hallows Parish Church, Twickenham, in 2002. Over 50 members of the congregation participated in the groups, which ran during a variety of days and times in homes around the parish.

As a result of the course a parish pastoral visiting team was set up with 12 members, who undertook electoral roll visiting, caring for members of the whole church community.

Appendix 2

SMART goals

S   Specific and stretching

- A goal should be specific in its aim and objectives.
- Work on producing the best wording will pay dividends in the long term.
- A goal should also take you on from your current situation.
- It shouldn't simply be a statement of what's already happening.

M   Measurable

- It is important to be able to see results and, in order do this, goals need to be measurable.
- Something vague like 'It would be good to see more people in church' is likely to cause disappointment. How many new people? By when?

A   Achievable and agreed

- Unachievable goals lead directly to guilt and anger.
- Also, make sure that there is consensus, and that it isn't just one person's – or a small group's – bright idea.

R   Relevant and realistic

- Make the goal relevant to each situation. Every church, every community is different. Just because the church down the road is doing something doesn't mean it will be right for you. It has to be your goal for your situation.
- Ensure, too, that it is realistic for your situation; nothing is more depressing than unrealistic goals.
- It can be good to include some early 'easy wins'. This will give encouragement to all involved in the process.

T Time-bound and timely

- Set a time by which the goal is to be achieved. Then, at that point, it can be either ticked off or reviewed.
- Fundraising thermometers outside a church, marked a tenth of the way up, with paint peeling off, are less than unhelpful and dreadful publicity!
- The timing of the goal should also be appropriate, in terms of what else is going on and what other priorities are set.

Notes

1 Introduction: Training and development that sticks

1 The research was a part of a doctoral thesis entitled 'Developing clergy: what does "continuing professional development" mean for Church of England clergy today?', 2010.

2 Whose agenda?

1 Michael Sadgrove (2008) *Wisdom and Ministry*, London: SPCK, p. 40.
2 <www.cpas.org.uk/events-and-programmes/equipping-leaders/arrow-leadership-programme>.
3 Compton International.
4 See CPAS Growing Leaders course, <www.cpas.org.uk/church-resources/growing-leaders-suite>.

3 Working below the surface

1 John Henry Newman (1994) *Apologia pro Vita Sua*, Harmondsworth: Penguin Classics (first published 1864).
2 See, for example, Potter (2009).
3 SMART is an acronym for effective planning which stands for Specific, Measurable, Achievable, Realistic and Time-bound (see Appendix 2). For more information on this and on Mission Action Planning in general, see <www.london.anglican.org/MAP> for free resources.
4 See, for example, Jackson (2005).
5 For further information on History Audit see <www.london.anglican.org/MAP> or <www.open.ac.uk/buildingonhistory/resource-guide/church-and-parish-history.htm>. A more detailed account is soon to be published as a Grove Booklet.
6 Warren (2004: Appendix 4).
7 See <www.appreciativeinquiry.cwru.edu>.
8 See <www.ncd-international.org>.
9 See <www.faithworks.info>.

10 See <www.london.anglican.org/MAP> *Introduction to Mission Action Planning.*
11 See Jackson (2004 and 2005).

4 Complementary approaches

1 See <www.cpas.org.uk>.
2 See Ken Blanchard and Paul Hersey (1979) *The Family Game,* Boston: Addison-Wesley; and Ken Blanchard, Robert H. Guest and Paul Hersey (1986) *Organizational Change through Effective Leadership,* New Jersey: Prentice Hall.
3 See <www.kenblanchard.com>.
4 Further information about the Hersey–Blanchard leadership model can be found at <www.mindtools.com/pages/article/newLDR_44.htm>. A more detailed account can be found in P. Hersey and K. H. Blanchard (1999) *Leadership and the One Minute Manager,* New York: William Morrow.
5 See <www.carlislediocese.org.uk/ministry-training-and-vocation/growing-as-christians/Shape.html>.

5 What am I like?

1 See <www.businessballs.com/kolblearningstyles.htm>.
2 Again, Lamdin and Tilley (2007) give a good account of Myers-Briggs.

6 Reflection and review

1 Neil Evans and Pete Broadbent (2007) *Diocesan Ministerial Development Review Scheme: Review panel report,* London: Diocese of London, p. 4.
2 See Appendix 2, p. 135.

7 Why shared ministry?

1 See, for example, the works of Boff, Gunton, Moltmann, Zizoulas, Paul Fiddes, and many others.

8 An integrated and structured approach

1 Stanley Hauerwas (1988) *Christian Existence Today,* New York: Labyrinth, p. 135.
2 Neil Evans (2006) 'Research into the effectiveness of the Ministerial Development Programme of the Diocese of London' (unpublished), King's College London; the themes are summarized at Appendix 5.
3 Jackson (2002, 2004 and 2005).

4 This can be found in many sources, but for quick reference see <www. businessballs.com/maslow.htm>. In this quick reference guide the author offers this summary of the five stages:

  (a) Biological and physiological needs – air, food, drink, shelter, warmth, sex, sleep, etc.
  (b) Safety needs – protection from elements, security, order, law, limits, stability, etc.
  (c) Belongingness and love needs – work group, family, affection, relationships, etc.
  (d) Esteem needs – self-esteem, achievement, mastery, independence, status, dominance, prestige, managerial responsibility, etc.
  (e) Self-actualization needs – realizing personal potential, self-fulfilment, seeking personal growth and peak experiences.

5 See discussion elsewhere, and including Kolb's four stages of learning (Kolb 1984) which offers four distinct learning styles (he suggests each person has a preference for one particular style), a development of his four-stage learning cycle. Honey and Mumford have usefully adapted these to: Activist, Reflector, Theorist and Pragmatist (most recently in Peter Honey and Alan Mumford (2000) *The Learning Styles Helper's Guide*, Coventry: Peter Honey Publications).

Bibliography

Adair, John (1987) *Effective Teambuilding*, London: Gower.

Adey, Philip (2004) *The Professional Development of Teachers: Practice and theory*, London: Kluwer.

Astley, Jeff (2007) *Christ of the Everyday*, London: SPCK.

Chew, Mike and Mark Ireland (2009) *How to Do Mission Action Planning*, London: SPCK.

de Mello, Anthony (1997) *The Heart of the Enlightened*, Oxford: Image Publishing.

Fiddes, Paul (2000) *Participating in God*, London: DLT.

Green, Laurie (2009) *Let's Do Theology*, London: Cassell, second edition (first edition 1989).

Greenwood, Robin (1994) *Transforming Priesthood*, London: SPCK.

Honey, Peter and Alan Mumford (1986) *The Manual of Learning Styles*, Coventry: Peter Honey Publications.

Hopewell, James (1987) *Congregation: Stories and structure*, Philadelphia: Fortress.

Jackson, Bob (2002) *Hope for the Church*, London: Church House Publishing.

Jackson, Bob (2004) *A Capital Idea*, London: Church House Publishing.

Jackson, Bob (2005) *The Road to Growth*, London: Church House Publishing.

Kolb, David (1984) *Experiential Learning: Experience as the source of learning and development*, New Jersey: Prentice Hall.

Lamdin, Keith and David Tilley (2007) *Supporting New Ministers in the Local Church*, London: SPCK.

Lee, Carl and Sarah Horsman (2002) *Affirmation and Accountability*, Exeter: Society of Mary and Martha.

Pedrick, Claire and Su Blanch (2011) *How to Make Great Appointments in the Church*, London: SPCK.

Percy, Martyn (2006) *Clergy: The origin of species*, London: T. & T. Clark.

Percy, Martyn and Ian Markham (eds) (2006) *Why Liberal Churches are Growing*, London: T. & T. Clark.

Potter, Phil (2009) *The Challenge of Change*, Abingdon: Bible Reading Fellowship.

Schön, Donald (1991) *The Reflective Practitioner*, Aldershot: Ashgate.

Warren, Rick (1995) *The Purpose Driven Church*, Grand Rapids, Michigan: Zondervan.

Warren, Robert (2004) *The Healthy Churches' Handbook*, London: Church House Publishing.

Wink, Walter (1984) *Naming the Powers*, Philadelphia: Augsburg Fortress.

Wink, Walter (1990) *Transforming Bible Study*, Nashville: Abingdon Press.